NEW
AND
SELECTED
POEMS
1923-1985

John Brown: The Making of a Martyr
Thirty-six Poems
Night Rider
Eleven Poems on the Same Theme
At Heaven's Gate
Selected Poems, 1923–1943
All the King's Men
Blackberry Winter
The Circus in the Attic
World Enough and Time
Brother to Dragons
Band of Angels
Segregation: The Inner Conflict in the South
Promises: Poems 1954–1956
Selected Essays
The Cave
All the King's Men (play)
You, Emperors, and Others: Poems 1957–1960
The Legacy of the Civil War
Wilderness
Flood
Who Speaks for the Negro?
Selected Poems: New and Old, 1923–1966
Incarnations: Poems 1966–1968
Audubon: A Vision
Homage to Theodore Dreiser
Meet Me in the Green Glen
Or Else—Poem/Poems 1968–1974
Democracy and Poetry
Selected Poems: 1923–1975
A Place to Come To
Now and Then: Poems 1976–1978
Brother to Dragons: A New Version
Being Here: Poetry 1977–1980
Jefferson Davis Gets His Citizenship Back
Rumor Verified: Poems 1979–1980
Chief Joseph of the Nez Perce
New and Selected Poems: 1923–1985

NEW
AND
SELECTED
POEMS,
1923-1985

Robert Penn Warren

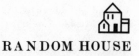

RANDOM HOUSE
NEW YORK

LIBRARY OF CONGRESS CATALOGING IN PUBLICATION DATA
Warren, Robert Penn, 1905–
New and selected poems, 1923–1985.
I. Title.
PS3545.A748A6 1985   811'.52   84–45755
ISBN 0–394–54380–7
ISBN 0–394–73848–9 (pbk.)
ISBN 0–394–54586–9 (lim ed.)

A signed first edition of this book has been privately printed
by The Franklin Library.

Manufactured in the United States of America
98765432
First Random House Edition

ACKNOWLEDGMENTS

The following poems were first published in *The New Yorker*:

"Where the Slow Fig's Purple Sloth," "Old Nigger on One-Mule Cart Encountered Late at Night When Driving Home from Party in the Back Country," "Little Black Heart of the Telephone," "Red-Tail Hawk and Pyre of Youth," "American Portrait: Old Style," "The Cross," "What Voice at Moth-Hour," "Looking Northward, Aegeanward: Nestlings on Seacliff," "Three Darknesses," "Caribou," "Far West Once," "Rumor at Twilight," "Literal Dream," "The Place," "It Is Not Dead," "New Dawn."

"Rumor Verified" was first published in *Antaeus*. "Evening Hawk" and "Midnight Outcry" were first published in *The Atlantic*. "Muted Music," "Why You Climbed Up," and "Seasons" were first published in *The Georgia Review*. "A Way to Love God" was first published in *The London Times*. "Arizona Midnight" and "Winter Wheat: Oklahoma" were first published in the *New England Review and Bread Loaf Quarterly*. "Paradox" was first published in *The New York Review of Books*.

Other poems were first published in the following publications: *The American Poetry Review*, *The Atlantic*, *Encounter*, *Forum*, *The Georgia Review*, *Grand Street*, *Harper's Magazine*, *Kentucky Poetry Review*, *The Kenyon Review*, *The Nation*, *New England Review and Bread Loaf Quarterly*, *The New Leader*, *The New York Review*, *The New York Review of Books*, *The Ohio Review*, *Partisan Review*, *Poetry*, *Quest/78*, *Salmagundi*, *Saturday Review*, *Scribner's Magazine*, *The Sewanee Review*, *The Southern Review*, *Times Literary Supplement*, *The Washington Post*, and *The Yale Review*.

CONTENTS

ALTITUDES AND EXTENSIONS 1980-1984

From CAN I SEE ARCTURUS FROM WHERE I STAND? Poems 1975

From OR ELSE — Poem/Poems 1968-1974

AUDUBON: A VISION

From INCARNATIONS Poems 1966-1968

From TALE OF TIME Poems 1960-1966

From YOU, EMPERORS, AND OTHERS
Poems 1957-1960

From PROMISES Poems 1954-1956

From SELECTED POEMS 1923-1943

ALTITUDES
AND EXTENSIONS
1980-1984

To our granddaughter, Katherine Penn Scully

Will ye not now after that life is descended
down to you, will not you ascend up to it
and live?

—St. Augustine: *Confessions*,
Book IV, Chapter XII
Translated by William Watts

* This symbol is used to indicate a space between sections of a poem wherever such spaces are lost in pagination.

I

Three Darknesses

I

There is some logic here to trace, and I
Will try hard to find it. But even as I begin, I
Remember one Sunday morning, festal with springtime, in
The zoo of Rome. In a natural, spacious, grassy area,
A bear, big as a grizzly, erect, indestructible,
Unforgiving as God, as rhythmic as
A pile-driver—right-left, right-left—
Slugged at an iron door. The door,
Heavy, bolted, barred, must have been
The entrance to a dark enclosure, a cave,
Natural or artificial. Minute by minute, near, far,
Wheresoever we wandered, all Sunday morning,
With the air full of colored balloons trying to escape
From children, the ineluctable
Rhythm continues. You think of the
Great paws like iron on iron. Can iron bleed?
Since my idiot childhood the world has been
Trying to tell me something. There is something
Hidden in the dark. The bear
Was trying to enter into the darkness of wisdom.

II

Up Black Snake River, at anchor in
That black tropical water, we see
The cormorant rise—cranky, graceless,
Ungeared, unhinged, one of God's more cynical
Improvisations, black against carmine of sunset. He
Beats seaward. The river gleams blackly west, and thus
The jungle divides on a milk-pale path of sky toward the sea.
Nothing human is visible. Each of us lies looking
Seaward. Ice melts in our glasses. We seem ashamed

Of conversation. Asia is far away. The radio is not on.
The grave of my father is far away. Our host
Rises silently, is gone. Later we see him,
White helmet in netting mystically swathed,
As he paddles a white skiff into the tangled
Darkness of a lagoon. There moss hangs. Later,
Dark now, we see the occasional stab of his powerful
Light back in the darkness of trunks rising
From the side lagoon, the darkness of moss suspended.
We think of the sound a snake makes
As it slides off a bough—the slop, the slight swish,
The blackness of water. You
Wonder what your host thinks about
When he cuts the light and drifts on the lagoon of midnight.
Though it is far from midnight. Upon his return,
He will, you know,
Lie on the deck-teak with no word. Your hostess
Had gone into the cabin. You hear
The pop of a wine cork. She comes back. The wine
Is breathing in darkness.

        III

The nurse is still here. Then
She is not here. You
Are here but are not sure
It is you in the sudden darkness. No matter.
A damned nuisance, but trivial—
The surgeon has just said that. A dress rehearsal,
You tell yourself, for
The real thing. Later. Ten years? Fifteen?
Tomorrow, only a dry run. At
5 A.M. they will come. Your hand reaches out in darkness
To the TV button. It is an old-fashioned western.
Winchester fire flicks white in the dream-night.
It has something to do with vice and virtue, and the vastness
Of moonlit desert. A stallion, white and flashing, slips,
Like spilled quicksilver, across
The vastness of moonlight. Black
Stalks of cacti, like remnants of forgotten nightmares, loom
Near at hand. Action fades into distance, but

You are sure that virtue will triumph. Far beyond
All the world, the mountains lift. The snow peaks
Float into moonlight. They float
In that unnamable altitude of white light. God
Loves the world. For what it is.

Mortal Limit

I saw the hawk ride updraft in the sunset over Wyoming.
It rose from coniferous darkness, past gray jags
Of mercilessness, past whiteness, into the gloaming
Of dream-spectral light above the last purity of snow-snags.

There—west—were the Tetons. Snow-peaks would soon be
In dark profile to break constellations. Beyond what height
Hangs now the black speck? Beyond what range will gold eyes see
New ranges rise to mark a last scrawl of light?

Or, having tasted that atmosphere's thinness, does it
Hang motionless in dying vision before
It knows it will accept the mortal limit,
And swing into the great circular downwardness that will restore

The breath of earth? Of rock? Of rot? Of other such
Items, and the darkness of whatever dream we clutch?

Immortality Over the Dakotas

It is not you that moves. It is the dark.
While you loll lax, semisomnolent, inside the great capsule,
Dark hurtles past. Now at the two-inch-thick plane-window glass,
You press your brow, see the furious
Futility of darkness boil past. It can't get in.
It is as though you were at last immortal.

You feel as though you had just had a quick dip
In the Lamb's mystic blood. You laugh into manic darkness.
You laugh at the tiny glow that far, far down
Shines like a glowworm beside an unseeable stone.
It would be a little Dakota town where
Population has not been dipped in the mystic blood.

On a July afternoon you once gassed up
At a town like that: movie, eatery, Baptist church
(Red brick), tourist court, white shotgun bungalows,
Wheat elevator towering over all.
Farms, of course, bleeding out forever.
Most likely the mercury stood at a hundred and one.

Now suddenly through glass, through dark fury, you see
Who must be down there, with collar up on the dirty sheepskin,
Snow on red hunter's cap, earflaps down.
Chores done. But he just can't bring himself to go in.
The doctor's just said he won't last till another winter.

She's sitting inside, white bun of hair neat as ever,
Squinting studiously down through bifocals at what she's knitting.
He knows her fire's getting low, but he can't go in.
He knows that if he did he might let something slip.
He couldn't stand that. So stares at the blackness of sky.
Stares at lights, green and red, that tread the dark of your immortality.

7

Caribou

Far, far southward, the forest is white, not merely
As snow of no blemish, but whiter than ice yet sharing
The mystic and blue-tinged, tangential moonlight,
Which in unshadowed vastness breathes northward.
Such great space must once
Have been a lake, now, long ages, ice-solid.

Shadows shift from the whiteness of forest, small
As they move on the verge of moon-shaven distance. They grow clear,
As binoculars find the hairline adjustment.
They seem to drift from the purity of forest.
Single, snow-dusted above, each shadow appears, each
Slowly detached from the white anonymity
Of forest, each hulk
Lurching, each lifted leg leaving a blackness as though
Of a broken snowshoe partly withdrawn. We know
That the beast's foot spreads like a snowshoe to support
That weight, that bench-kneed awkwardness.

The heads heave and sway. It must be with spittle
That jaws are ice-bearded. The shoulders
Lumber on forward, as though only the bones could, inwardly,
Guess destination. The antlers,
Blunted and awkward, are carved by some primitive craftsman.

We do not know on what errand they are bent, to
What mission committed. It is a world that
They live in, and it is their life.
They move through the world and breathe destiny.
Their destiny is as bright as crystal, as pure
As a dream of zero. Their destiny
Must resemble happiness even though
They do not know that name.

*

I lay the binoculars on the lap of the biologist. He
Studies distance. The co-pilot studies a map. He glances at
A compass. At mysterious dials. I drink coffee. Courteously,
The binoculars come back to me.

I have lost the spot. I find only blankness.

                                        But
They must have been going somewhere.

The First Time

Northwest Montana, high country, and downward
The trail, not man-made, too narrow, with boughs
Snatching blue-jean thighs, stubs scraping
At boots. "Hold it!" Old Jack said. Said: "Look!" Backward
Pointed. "Hot elk-turd," he said. "Ain't too many now.
Next cattle come in, then folks, and next
All hellebaloo." Added: "Done come down
For water at sunset. Hold back."

We held.
And soon see upstream the sandbar,
Each elk walking out to its depth, each one
Standing calm in leg riffles, head bowed
Against current, the pale patch of rump
Showing clear in late light, a snort
Now and then, spray bright.

                              One great bull,
Six cows, one young. "Gal season," Old Jack says,
"Nigh now. Rounden up his take, but now
Just a starter—him the feller he is.
Just look at that rack ride his head in the river.
Now ain't he a pisser!"

                    The pisser
Heaves up the far bank. Then he, the great one,
Stands back as though to take count. "That rack,"
Jack says, "he'll git it all ready and polished afore
The first fool young he-elk cuts in."

                    Now,
All up the willows and scrub-brush, but yet
He waits, head erect, profiled
Against snow of a far range, dark bull-cape

10

Of shoulders now seeming much darker, architecture of antlers,
Above the last line of the far snow, now sharp against sky,
Balanced and noble, with prongs
Thrust into the bronze-red sky as though,
On prong-tangs, to sustain, in that bronze-tinged emptiness, the massive
Sun-ball of flame, now swathed slightly in blue. The sun
Has touched snow before he turns.

That night,
On a broad sand patch at the head of the sandbar, we camped.
I woke in the night, at some distant howl. I saw
Stars immensely reflected in the quiet water. I had never seen
A bull wapiti, wild, before—the
Great head lifted in philosophic
Arrogance against
God's own sky.

Minnesota Recollection

By 3 P.M. the pat of snow-pads had begun
To cling to the windowpane, and in the old kitchen,
Daylight already a dream of dying, the color
Of water sloshed in a used milk can to clean
It. The hired girl
Shook each tin lamp to find it full, or

No. "Not dark as this," Old Grammy, in his musical tangle of
Never-learned English and quite unforgotten Swedish,
Said, "when it took all
We was to haul Old Ma down to the kitchen so
She could die more cheerful, not grave-cold
Between the sheets, and her not yet gone dead."
Who wants to die in a bed already
Colder than frozen ground they'll have to take
Pickaxes to get you into?

Sudden Old Sugfred—Grammy—was gone—or seemed so:
Like sometimes he could be so still, like not there, but
Now two tin lamps were lit, and you could see. He might
Just step outside to the call of nature, and once out,
See snowflakes falling, falling, and ponder on it a half-hour,
Making no move, sunk deep in the world, like a part
Of God's own world, a post, a bare tree, dung heap, or stone.
Gone to the barn, they guessed. *Yes, somebody's got to do it.*
Yeah, cattle's got rights, and if you got cattle,
They's due to be fed and bedded, and the old ax-butt
To bust the ice on the drinking trough.

They piled more wood, heard the clock say what
It would be saying till Earth's last breath: *tick*-and-*tock*.
But what they heard wasn't what they hoped to hear.
Somebody saw the new lantern on its nail.
Done took an old one, Gertie thought. *Or took*

12

His toy. The big flashlight—they called it that,
He loved it so. Then Gertie gone, soon back.
One hand holding an old lantern, lighted, the other
Old Grammy's toy—but it dead
As a monstrous catfish eye. He'd played
With it too much. No word she said, just screamed.
Her mackinaw just half-jerked on, and screaming, she
Ran out. They did not seem to hear. But felt
It in their throats. The scream
Ran out the open door, darker
Than Death. They lighted lanterns, both lanterns,
Then ran, somebody with the new one. Somebody
Stopped to shut the door. Somebody's
Got to think of that.

In the barn nobody. Ice not cracked. Then outside—
But what are lanterns in a world so wide! Somebody
Fell, and something's broken, one last flare. Worse—
Who could see the window now?
They scattered, trying to see, calling, calling
The name they searched for, or
Simply calling as though the window had a voice to answer.
And suddenly another lantern's gone. It's dry.

If there's one spot, however frail, yet left of hope—
But what can a last lantern do? Oh, the world is wide.
They tried to make a chain of calls, a rope
To hold the human hope together. Oh, why
Is darkness from white snow the darkest thing yet?
Somebody fell in slack blackness. It must
Have felt like a gift. Will tomorrow be
Like today? And was today so goddamned sweet?

Just tell me that.

But suddenly a call again. In last despair?
But then one more. And more, until
The human chain's about to fill the night,
With throats blood-washed and foaming
As the breathed air is knife-edge to suffering past grief.

*

13

Then one last call. "The window!"—it said, or seemed to say.
So voices again picked up
The gnarled, untwisting length of rope
Of human hope.

Back at the house one last log faintly glowed.
More wood. Then each sits as before.
Till Gertie screams, tries to run.
They held her down. Then all sit as before.
But one. But he—he fills their heads all night.
He filled the room.

***

By first flame of the prairie dawn they found him.
Snagged on a barbed-wire fence that he'd
Followed the wrong way, hearing no voices, maybe.
At least a mile. His face was calm.
It had, you might say, an innocent expression.

Arizona Midnight

The grief of the coyote seems to make
Stars quiver whiter over the blankness which
Is Arizona at midnight. In sleeping-bag,
Protected by the looped rampart of anti-rattler horsehair rope,
I take a careful twist, grinding sand on sand,
To lie on my back. I stare. Stars quiver, twitch,
In their infinite indigo. I know
Nothing to tell the stars, who go,
Age on age, along tracks they understand, and
The only answer I have for the coyote would be
My own grief, for which I have no
Tongue—indeed, scarcely understand.
Eastward, I see
No indication of dawn, not yet ready for the scream
Of inflamed distance,
Which is the significance of day.
But dimly I do see
Against that darkness, lifting in blunt agony,
The single great cactus. Once more I hear the coyote
Wail. I strain to make out the cactus. It has
Its own necessary beauty.

Far West Once

Aloud, I said, with a slight stir of heart,
"The last time"—and thought, years thence, to a time
When only in memory I might
Repeat this last tramp up the shadowy gorge
In the mountains, cabinward, the fall
Coming on, the aspen leaf gold, sun low
At the western end of the gun-barrel passage
Waiting, waiting the trigger-touch
And the blast of darkness—the target me.

I said, "I'll try to remember as much
As a man caught in Time cannot forget,"
For I carried a headful of summer, and knew
That I'd never again, in the gloaming, walk
Up that trail, now lulled by the stone-song of waters;
Nor again on path pebbles, noon-plain, see
The old rattler's fat belly twist and distend
As it coiled, and the rattles up from dust rise
To vibrate mica-bright, in the sun's beam;
Nor again, from below, on the cliff's over-thrust,
Catch a glimpse of the night-crouching cougar's eyes
That, in my flashlight's strong beam, had burned
Coal-bright as they swung,
Detached, contemptuous, and slow,
Into the pine woods' mounting mass
Of darkness that, eventually,
Ahead, would blot out, star by star,
The slot of the sky-slice that now I
Moved under, and on to dinner and bed.

And to sleep—and even in sleep to feel
The nag and pretensions of day dissolve
And flow away in that musical murmur
Of waters; then to wake in dark with some strange

Heart-hope, undefinable, verging to tears
Of happiness and the soul's calm.

How long ago! But in years since,
On other trails, in the shadow of
What other cliffs, in lands with names
Crank on the tongue, I have felt my boots
Crush gravel, or press the soundlessness
Of detritus of pine or fir, and heard
Movement of water, far, how far—

Or waking under nameless stars,
Have heard such redemptive music, from
Distance to distance threading starlight,
Able yet, as long ago,
Despite scum of wastage and scab of years,
To touch again the heart, as though at a dawn
Of dew-bright Edenic promise, with,
Far off, far off, in verdurous shade, first birdsong.

II

Rumor at Twilight

Rumor at twilight of whisper, crepuscular
Agitation, from no quarter defined, or something
Like the enemy fleet below the horizon, in
Its radio blackout, unobserved. In a dark cave,
Dark fruit, bats hang. Droppings
Of generations, soft underfoot, would carpet the gravel—
That is, if you came there again. Have you ever felt,
Between thumb and forefinger, texture
Of the bat's wing? Their hour soon comes.

You stand in the dark, under the maples, digesting
Dinner. You have no particular
Financial worries, just nags. Your children
Seem to respect you. Your wife is kind. Fireflies
Punctuate the expensive blackness of shrubbery,
Their prickling glows—here, there—like the phosphorescent
Moments of memory when, in darkness, your head first
Dents the dark pillow, eyes wide, ceilingward.
Can you really reconstruct your mother's smile?

You stand in the dark, heart even now filling, and think of
A boy who, drunk with the perfume of elder blossoms
And the massiveness of moonrise, stood
In a lone lane, and cried out,
In a rage of joy, to seize, and squeeze, significance from,
What life is, whatever it is. Now
High above the maples the moon presides. The first bat
Mathematically zigzags the stars. You fling down
The cigarette butt. Set heel on it. It is time to go in.

Old Dog Dead

Cocker. English. Fifteen years old. Tumor
Of testes. Vet promising nothing. So did it.

Inevitable, but inevitable, too, the
Recollection of the first time, long back,
Seen—puppy-whirl
Of flopping forepaws, flopping ears oversize, stub
Tail awag, eyes bright. And brighter yet,
Dancing in joy-light, the eyes
Of a little girl with her new love. Holding
It up to show. That was what my eyes, open in darkness,
Had now just seen.

And what, no doubt, the eyes now closed beside me
Had, too, been seeing in darkness. With no confirmation needed
To pass between. And now
That breath beside me was at last
Even in sleep. I thought of the possible time
When evenness—in what ears?—
Might be of silence
Only.

Fingering familiar dark, I made
My way out.

2

Boots on, pullover over
Night shirt, on shoulders camp blanket,
Barberry-ripped—whatever
Came handy in anteroom. Then,
I was standing in starlight, moon

19

Long since behind the mountain, mountain blackness at my back.
On mossed stone sitting, I, streamward,
Stare, intent
On the stream's now messageless murmur of motion.

The stars are high-hung, clearly
Defined in night's cloudlessness,
But here, below, identity blurred
In the earth-bound waver of water.

Upward again I look. See Jupiter, contemptuous,
Noble, firmly defined,
The month being June, the place Vermont.

    3

I shut eyes and see what
I had not in actuality seen—the
Raw earth, red clay streaked with
Black of humus under
The tall pine, anonymous in
The vet's woodlot.

Will I ever go back there? Absurdly,
I think I might go and put, stuck in the clay,
A stone—any stone large enough. No word, just something
To make a change, however minute,
In the structure of the universe.

    4

I think of Pharaoh's
Unblinking gaze across
Sands endless.

If we can think of timelessness, does it exist?

    5

Now Jupiter, southwest, beyond the sagging black spur
Of the mountain, in the implacable

Mathematics of a planet,
Has set. Tell me,
Is there a garden where
The petal, dew-kissed, withereth not?
And where, in darkness, beyond what bramble and flint,
Would iron gate, on iron hinge, move without sound?

Far off, a little girl, little no longer, would,
If yet she knew,
Lie in her bed and weep
For what life is.

6

Who will be the last to remember tonight?

Perhaps, far off, long later, an old woman,
Who once was the child,
Now alone, waking before dawn to fumble for
Something she painfully knows but cannot lay hand to, in
The unlabeled detritus and trash of Time.

Hope

In the orchidaceous light of evening
Watch how, from the lowest hedge-leaf, creeps,
Grass blade to blade, the purpling shadow. It spreads
Its spectral ash beneath the leveling, last
Gold rays that, westward, have found apertures
From the magnificent disaster of the day.

Against gold light, beneath the maple leaf,
A pale blue gathers, accumulates, sifts
Downward to modulate the flowery softness
Of gold intrusive through the blackening spruce boughs.
Spruces heighten the last glory beyond by their stubbornness.
They seem rigid in blackened bronze.

Wait, wait—as though a finger were placed to lips.
The first star petals timidly in what
Is not yet darkness. That audacity
Will be rewarded soon. In this transitional light,
While cinders in the west die, the world
Has its last blooming. Let your soul

Be still. All day it has curdled in your bosom
Denatured by intrusion of truth or lie, or both.
Lay both aside, nor debate their nature. Soon,
While not even a last bird twitters, the last bat goes.
Even the last motor fades into distance. The promise
Of moonrise will dawn, and slowly, in all fullness, the moon

Will dominate the sky, the world, the heart,
In white forgiveness.

Why You Climbed Up

Where, vomit-yellow, the lichen crawls
Up the boulder, where the rusty needle
Falls from the pine to pad earth's silence
Against what intrusive foot may come, you come—
But come not knowing where or why.
Like substance hangs the silence of
The afternoon. Look—you will see
The tiny glint of the warbler's eye, see
The beak, half-open, in still heat gasp, see
Moss on a cliff, where water oozes.

Where or why,
You wonder, wandering, with sweat and pant,
Up the mountain's heave and clamber,
As though to forget and leave
All things, great and small, you call
The past, all things, great and small, you call
The Self, and remember only how once
In the moonlit Pacific you swam west, hypnotized
By stroke on stroke, the rhythm that
Filled all the hollow head and was
The only self you carried with you then.

What brought you back?
You can't remember now,
And do not guess that years from now you may not remember
How once—now—on this high ridge, seeing
The sun blaze down on the next and higher horizon,
You turned, and bumbled for some old logging road
To follow, stumbling, down.

Then all begins again. And you are you.

Literal Dream

(Twenty Years After Reading Tess *and*
Without Ever Having Seen Movie)

You know the scene. You read it in a book.
But did not see what I saw when,
Last night, unseen, I sat, and saw
The bare and tidy room, gone chilly too,
In its English respectability of straitened means.
She rocked in her chair, the old lady,
Bifocals, hair in a bun, neat, gray-streaked, the only
Sound the click of the knitting needles. She
So sat, alone, not seeing me, probably
Just seeing the empty chair I sat in, breath
Soundless. If there was breath. Do we,
Under such circumstances, breathe? When,
Transparent, we sit? She rocked and thought.

Oh, I could read her like the book I'd read!
How handy now came the paying guests
In the room upstairs. A widow
Has to cut her corners when she can.
I knew what she'd picked up. I waited.
Watched. It seemed she'd never look up and see
What I knew she'd see up there. But according to
The law of such circumstances, I
Could not look up until she did. She did.

She saw the ceiling spot. Ignored it. Looked
Again. Now bigger, darker, growing, it was
On paint, on whitewash, on paper, whatever
The ceiling was. I can't remember, but
Remember it growing slow, so slow. Her eyes,
They widened in hynotic slowness.
Her breath, it didn't come until
The stain on her neat ceiling gathered to a
Point.

24

Which hung forever.
Dropped.

How long would it now take for the tremble
Of finger to sharpen into the instrument
To touch
The spot now on the clean floor? It seemed
Forever. The knitting needles first,
Then the ball of wool, unnoticed, dropped. And then,
The finger, sharpening in massive will,
Suddenly no quivering,
Touched.

It rose.

How slow, how unbelieving, head
Shaking on frail stem of neck, she
Stared.

Her mouth had now made the shape of an *O*.
But no sound came. I stared to see
The shape of sound. It was not there.

I could not make out the color of the stained finger.
But knew. I knew because I'd read the book.
But the blind swirl of eyeless cloud,
Tattered, black-streaked,
In which, that instant, I was up-whirled,
Was in no book, nor ever had been, nor
Such terror.

I woke at the call of nature. It was near day.
Patient I sat, staring through the
Wet pane at sparse drops that struck
The last red dogwood leaves. It was as though
I could hear the plop there. See the leaf quiver.

After the Dinner Party

You two sit at the table late, each, now and then,
Twirling a near-empty wine glass to watch the last red
Liquid climb up the crystalline spin to the last moment when
Centrifugality fails: with nothing now said.

What is left to say when the last logs sag and wink?
The dark outside is streaked with the casual snowflake
Of winter's demise, all guests long gone home, and you think
Of others who never again can come to partake

Of food, wine, laughter, and philosophy—
Though tonight one guest has quoted a killing phrase we owe
To a lost one whose grin, in eternal atrophy,
Now in dark celebrates some last unworded jest none can know.

Now a chair scrapes, sudden, on tiles, and one of you
Moves soundless, as in hypnotic certainty,
The length of table. Stands there a moment or two,
Then sits, reaches out a hand, open and empty.

How long it seems till a hand finds that hand there laid,
While ash, still glowing, crumbles, and silence is such
That the crumbling of ash is audible. Now naught's left unsaid
Of the old heart-concerns, the last, tonight, which

Had been of the absent children, whose bright gaze
Over-arches the future's horizon, in the mist of your prayers.
The last log is black, while ash beneath displays
No last glow. You snuff candles. Soon the old stairs

Will creak with your grave and synchronized tread as each mounts
To a briefness of light, then true weight of darkness, and then
That heart-dimness in which neither joy nor sorrow counts.
Even so, one hand gropes out for another, again.

Doubleness in Time

Doubleness coils in Time like
The bull-snake in fall's yet-leafed growth. *Then*
Uncoils like *Now. Now*
Like *Then*. Oh, it
Was long ago—the years, how many?
Fifty—but now at last it truly
Happens. Only *Now*. Her eyes,

From one to another of those who
Stand by, move. You hear,
Almost, the grind in the socket.
The face fixes on each face, and for
Each face constructs
A smile. You hear,
Almost, the grind of the smile
Being manufactured, bit by bit. You hear
The grind of love.

You hear the grind of the smile as you try to smile.

Her eyes, after each effort, fix
On the ceiling of white plaster above them. The pink
Of sunset tints the ceiling. I stare
At the ceiling. It is Infinity.

It roofs all Time.

From his vest pocket the doctor draws
Out the old-fashioned gold-cased watch.
You hear the click as it opens.
Your heart stands still as a stone.
He holds her pulse.

He nods. Slowly. Slowly.

*

My father, that tall, thin man,
Head sculptured bald and white as marble,
Great Roman nose—he moves first.
He leans above the waiting upturned face.
Lips are laid—you know they are cold—to lips.
Hand touches hand.
I am seeing that *Now*.

By downward age, each child there repeats the act.
The youngest last.

The door opens. Is shut.
The doctor remains within. The nurse
Is no more than an advertising dummy
In a store window.

The little boy in the hall lingers last, is lost.
"Oh, I'm by myself," his voice cries out.

To the waiting room the boy comes.
No word. My father
Sits rigid on a bench. His loneliness
Is what he seems to insist on. As though
He were stone, white stone beneath dark cloth.
It is as though an antique statue,
Exhumed after centuries, were
In modern costume dressed. Why
Didn't I laugh *Then*? I
Feel like laughing *Now*.

His eyes show nothing.
Like stone, too.

The doctor comes in. Nods.

Soundlessly, as though from an ax-butt
Set sudden to temple, the tall man falls
Rigid. Sidewise.

His daughter stoops to hold his rigid hand.

*

At last, he kisses her hand. Rises:
Face severe, nost out-thrust. Eyes
Glittering, cold.
In dignity shakes hands with the doctor.
Joins him in the hall.

I stand on the gravel of the parking lot, alone.
It is not *Then*.
It is *Now*. For it
Has taken a long time for Truth to become true.

It is autumn, *Now* as *Then*, and the stars
Have begun their wintry tingle.
The moon is full, white, but
Westering above black roofs
Of the little city.
People live there.

I stare at the moon,
And wonder why it has never moved all these years.
I do not know why, nor know
Why my grief has not been understood, nor why
It has not understood its own being.

It takes a long time for it to learn
Its many names: like
Selfishness and *Precious Guilt*.

Snowfall

The whiteness of silence, in silence of squadrons
Of cottony hooves, no creaking of stirrup, no steel-flash—
Over my western hill the white cavalry comes
To blot the last dying crimson that outlines the slope.
Was there a bugle? Or only wind in the spruces?
In the world what music may be that we cannot hear?

Years pass, and always so much to remember, forget: the first
Green to spring in green turf advertising
Earth's old immortality; the first
Whistle of blackbirds, or redwings, arriving,
Numberless, bubbling with music and sperm;
The first time your young face, shame-flushed, looked away
As she leaned hard against the fence-palings between you,
And pressed her new breasts to rise up.

Try hard to remember her name. What was it?
Try hard to remember the eye-gleam, the charming stupidity.

Think how slow was one afternoon's summer swell—
Like swelling of grape, apple, plum—as you lay alone on the hill,
And only the pure opalescence of sky
Filled eye and heart, and all you needed to know
Was the voicelessness you then lay in. But
Afternoons end. But later, remember
The hand you held in late shadow of beeches,
At the hour when no bird-call again comes.

Remember, remember "goodbye" on the station platform—and
Goodbye slips away like a snake in weed-tangle,
For the world is wide and has many phases and faces,
And the end of each summer is autumn's fruit.
What year will you know the fruit that is yourself?

*

The autumn bends with weight glossy and red.
The fat grape bleeds on the tongue, juice and pulp seeking
The throat's dark joy. You will walk again where chestnuts fall,
Dreaming that you, years back, a child, were happy there.

Meanwhile, far north in Vermont
Maples burn in last gold. When leaves fall the gray
Mountain ledges are noble. Deer
Graze where they now can. The bear
Will soon sleep with no dream. The trivial
Snow-swirl now there settles to business, the wind
Rises. Mantled in white,
Southward, two states, it strikes all the miles to the Sound,
Where, as you walk the salt-crusted sand, snowflakes
Die on the bay-swirl of small whitecaps.

And salt-crusted sand, under bootsole, creaks.

You do not remember what year was the first,
For many a year has passed. But now, again hillward,
Comes silence of cottony hooves, the wheeling of squadrons,
That tramp out last embers of day, and you

Stand in the darkness of whiteness
Which is the perfection of Being.

III

New Dawn

To John Hersey and Jacob Lawrence

1. EXPLOSION: SEQUENCE AND SIMULTANEITY

Greenwich Time	*11:16 P.M.*	August 5	1945
New York Time	*6:16 P.M.*	August 5	1945
Chicago Time	*5:16 P.M.*	August 5	1945
San Francisco Time	*3:16 P.M.*	August 5	1945
Pearl Harbor Time	*1:16 P.M.*	August 5	1945
Tinian Island Time	*9:16 A.M.*	August 6	1945
Hiroshima Time	*8:16 A.M.*	August 6	1945

2. GOODBYE TO TINIAN

Now that all the "unauthorized items" are cleared from the
                                        bomber, including
The optimistic irrelevance of six packs
Of condoms, and three pairs of
Pink silk panties. Now that
The closed briefing session of midnight
Is over, with no information from Colonel Tibbets, commander, on the
Secret, obsessive question of every crewman—What
Is the cargo? From Tibbets only
That it is "very powerful." Now that
The crew, at the end of the briefing,
Have taken what comfort they can from the prayer
Of their handsome chaplain, a man's man of
Rich baritone—"Almighty Father,
Who wilt hear the prayer of them that love Thee,
We pray Thee to be with those
Who brave the heights
Of Thy heaven..."

*

32

And now that around the bomber the klieg lights
Murdering darkness, the flashbulbs, the barking
Of cameramen, the anonymous faces preparing to be famous,
The nag of reporters, the handshakes, the jokes,
The manly embraces,
The scrape of city shoes on asphalt, the tarmac,
The news
From weather scouts out that clouds hovering over
The doomed world will, at dawn,
Probably clear. And,
Now down to brass tacks, Lewis,
The flawless co-pilot,
Addresses the crew, ". . . just don't
Screw it up. Let's do this really great!"

3. TAKE-OFF: TINIAN ISLAND

Colonel Tibbets, co-pilot beside him,
Lays hand to controls of the plane, which he
Has named for his mother, Enola Gay.

Pocketed secretly in Tibbets' survival vest,
Under the pale green coverall, is the
Metal container of twelve capsules of cyanide,
These for distribution to command if facing capture.

Though a heavy-caliber sidearm would serve.

The tow jeep strains at the leash. Wheels,
Under the weight of 150,000 pounds,
Overweight 15,000, crunch
Off the apron, bound for the runway. Position taken.

"This is Dimples Eighty-two to
North Tinian Tower. Ready for
Takeoff instructions."

So that is her name now. At least in code. Dimples.

"Tower to Dimples Eighty-two. Clear
To taxi. Take off Runway A, for Able."

*

At 2:45 A.M., August 6, Tinian Time,
Tibbets to Lewis:
"Let's go!"

All throttles full,
She roars down the runway, flicking past
Avenues of fire trucks, ambulances, overload
The last gamble, the runway
Now spilling furiously toward
Black sea-embrace.

Who would not have trusted the glittering record of Tibbets?

But even Lewis cries out. Grabs at controls. Tibbets,
Gaze fixed, hears nothing. Time
Seems to die. But
Iron hands, iron nerves, tighten at last, and
The control is drawn authoritatively back. The carriage
Rises to show
The air-slick belly where death sleeps.

This at cliff-verge.

Below, white, skeletal hands of foam
Grope up. Strain up.

Are empty.

4. MYSTIC NAME

Some 600 miles north-northwest to Iwo Jima, where,
In case of defect developing in the *Enola Gay*,
Tibbets will land, transfer cargo to
The waiting standby plane,
And take over. If not necessary,
No landing, but he will rendezvous
With weather planes and two B-29's
To fly with him as observers.

*

At 3 A.M., well short of Iwo Jima, code lingo
To Tinian Tower: "Judge going to work"—
To announce innocently the arming
Of the cargo. The cargo,
Inert as a sawed-off tree trunk ten feet long,
Twenty-eight inches in diameter, four and a half tons in weight, lies
In its dark covert.

It is
So quiet, so gentle as it rocks
In its dark cradle, in namelessness. But some
Name it "The Beast," and some,
With what irony, "Little Boy." Meanwhile,
It sleeps, with its secret name
And nature.

Like the dumb length of tree trunk, but literally
A great rifle barrel packed with uranium,
Two sections, forward one large, to rear one small, the two
Divided by a "tamper" of neutron-resistant alloy.
All harmless until, backed by vulgar explosive, the small will
Crash through to
The large mass
To wake it from its timeless drowse. And that
Will be that. Whatever
That may be.

5 . W H E N ?

When can that be known? Only after
The delicate and scrupulous fingers of "Judge"
Have done their work. After:
 1. Plugs, identified by the color green,
    Are installed in waiting sockets
 2. Rear plate is removed
 3. Armor plate is removed
 4. Breech wrench frees breech plug
 5. Breech plug is placed on rubber mat
 6. Explosive charge is reinserted,
    Four units, red ends to breech

35

7. Breech plug is reinserted, tightened home
8. Firing line is connected
9. Armor plate is reinstalled
10. Rear plate is reinstalled
11. Tools are removed
12. Catwalk is secured

In that dark cramp of tunnel, the precise
Little flashlight beam
Finicks, fastidious, over all.

Soft feet withdraw.

Later, 6:30 A.M. Japanese Time, last lap to target, green plugs
On the log, with loving care, tenderly, quietly
As a thief, will be replaced by plugs marked
Lethally red.

6. IWO JIMA

Over Iwo Jima, the moon, now westering, sinks in faint glimmer
Of horizon clouds. Soon
The heartbreaking incandescence of tropic dawn,
In which the *Enola Gay* loiters for contact
With weather scouts and the two B-29's
Which rise to attend her: observers.

Weather reports good from spotters.
Three options: Nagasaki, Kokura, Hiroshima.

But message of one spotter:
"Advise bombing primary"—i.e.,
Hiroshima.

Already preferred by Tibbets.

What added satisfaction it would have been to know that
At 7:31 A.M. Japanese Time, the
All Clear signal sounds over Hiroshima.

7. SELF AND NON-SELF

Tibbets looks down, sees
The slow, gray coiling of clouds, which are,
Beyond words, the image
Of sleep just as consciousness goes. He looks up, sees
Stars still glaring white down into
All the purity of emptiness. For an instant,
He shuts his eyes.

Shut
Your own eyes, and in timelessness you are
Alone with yourself. You are
Not certain of identity.
Has that non-self lived forever?

Tibbets jerks his eyes open. There
Is the world.

8. DAWN

Full dawn comes. Movement begins
In the city below. People
May even copulate. Pray. Eat. The sun
Offers its circular flame, incomparable,
Worship-worthy.

9. THE APPROACH

Speed 200 miles per hour, altitude
31,060 feet, directly toward the
Target control point of Aioi Bridge. On time. On
Calculation. Polaroid glasses
(Against brilliance of expected explosion)
Ordered on. Color
Of the world changes. It
Changes like a dream.

10. WHAT THAT IS

What clouds remain part now, magically,
And there visible, sprawling supine, unfended, the city.
The city opens itself, opening
As in breathless expectancy.

Crossed hairs of bombsight approach
Aioi Bridge as specified, on time
For the target. Ferebee, bombardier, presses
Forehead devoutly to the cushion of bombsight.
Says, "I've got it."

The bomb is activated:
Self-controlled for the six-mile earthward
Plunge—and at that instant the plane,
Purged of its burden, leaps upward,
As though in joy, and the bomb
Will reach the calculated optimum of distance
Above ground, 1,890
Feet, the altitude determined
By the bomb's own delicate brain.

There,
The apocalyptic blaze of
New dawn

Bursts.

Temperature at heart of fireball:
50,000,000 degrees centigrade.

Hiroshima Time: 8:16 A.M., August 6, 1945.

11. LIKE LEAD

Of that brilliance beyond brilliance, Tibbets
Was later to report: "A taste like lead."

12. MANIC ATMOSPHERE

Now, after the brilliance,
Suddenly, blindly, the plane
Heaves, is tossed
Like a dry leaf in
The massive and manic convulsion of
Atmosphere, which, compressed, from
Earth, miles down,

Bounces.

The plane recovers.

Again, then, the heave, the tossing.

With recovery.

13. TRIUMPHAL BEAUTY

Now, far behind, from the center of
The immense, purple-streaked, dark mushroom that, there, towers
To obscure whatever lies below,
A plume, positive but delicate as a dream,
Of pure whiteness, unmoved by breath of any wind,
Mounts.

Above the dark mushroom,
It grows high—high, higher—
In its own triumphal beauty.

14. HOME

Later, home. Tinian is man's only home—
The brotherly hug, the bear-embrace, the glory, and
"We made it!"

The music, then solemn
Silence of the pinning of the medal,
The mutual salute. At last,

The gorging of the gorgeous feast
To the point of vomit, the slosh
Of expensive alcohol
In bellies expensively swollen.

I 5 . SLEEP

Some men, no doubt, will, before sleep, consider
One thought: I am alone. But some,
In the mercy of God, or booze, do not

Long stare at the dark ceiling.

IV

The Distance Between: Picnic of Old Friends

In innocence, and nothing much to remember,
They wandered the green woodland lane,
All others behind them, friends, husband, wife,
And small children who sang
Beside the small tumult of white, singing water,
The picnic now over. They wandered
Deeper and deeper, in purposelessness,
Drifting like breath, more aimless and aimless, old words
Repeating old episodes, old shadows, the drift
Of childhood and years, all the shadowy
Uncoil of Time. All this—

While higher the sky now seemed to withdraw,
And higher rose beeches, then pines.
Till calmly they came
To the glen, where moss-streaked and noble, great cliffs
From ferns rose, and no bird sang. Ten feet
Apart they stopped. Stood. Each fearing
The sudden silence too much to lift eyes.

Of a sudden, she stared. Watched that face, stark and strange, moving,
Through distance, at her.

No resistance: seizure, penetration.

She sat in the rich, sap-bleeding, wild tangle of fern, and wept.
He stood by a beech, some twenty feet off, head down.

After what repair seemed possible, back they wandered,
The path and the world all strange, infinite
The distance between them.

At last, to the others, now starlit, they straggled, straggling
Toward song in the distance.

They tried to sing, too.

True Love

In silence the heart raves. It utters words
Meaningless, that never had
A meaning. I was ten, skinny, red-headed,

Freckled. In a big black Buick,
Driven by a big grown boy, with a necktie, she sat
In front of the drugstore, sipping something

Through a straw. There is nothing like
Beauty. It stops your heart. It
Thickens your blood. It stops your breath. It

Makes you feel dirty. You need a hot bath.
I leaned against a telephone pole, and watched.
I thought I would die if she saw me.

How could I exist in the same world with that brightness?
Two years later she smiled at me. She
Named my name. I thought I would wake up dead.

Her grown brothers walked with the bent-knee
Swagger of horsemen. They were slick-faced.
Told jokes in the barbershop. Did no work.

Their father was what is called a drunkard.
Whatever he was he stayed on the third floor
Of the big white farmhouse under the maples for twenty-five years.

He never came down. They brought everything up to him.
I did not know what a mortgage was.
His wife was a good, Christian woman, and prayed.

*

When the daughter got married, the old man came down wearing
An old tail coat, the pleated shirt yellowing.
The sons propped him. I saw the wedding. There were

Engraved invitations, it was so fashionable. I thought
I would cry. I lay in bed that night
And wondered if she would cry when something was done to her.

The mortgage was foreclosed. That last word was whispered.
She never came back. The family
Sort of drifted off. Nobody wears shiny boots like that now.

But I know she is beautiful forever, and lives
In a beautiful house, far away.
She called my name once. I didn't even know she knew it.

Last Walk of Season

For the last time, for this or perhaps
Any year to come in unpredictable life, we climb,
In the westward hour, up the mountain trail
To see the last light. Now
No cloud in the washed evening lours,
Though, under drum-tight roof, while each minute's
Mouse-tooth all night gnawed,
The season's first rain had done duty. Dams and traps,
Where the old logging trucks had once made tracks, now gurgle. That
Is the only voice we hear. We do not ask
What burden that music bears.

Our wish is to think of nothing but happiness. Of only
The world's great emptiness. How bright,
Rain-washed, the pebbles shine! A few high leaves
Of birch have golden gone. Ah, the heart leaps
That soon all earth will be of gold:
Gold birch, gold beech, gold maple. That
Is its own delight. Later, nothing visible
Except black conifers will clamber
Up the first white of ridge, then the crag's blank sun-blaze of snow.
Can it be that the world is but the great word
That speaks the meaning of our joy?

We came where we had meant to come. And not
Too late. In the mountain's cup, moraine-dammed, the lake
Lies left by a glacier older than God. Beyond it, the sun,
Ghostly, dips, flame-huddled in mist. We undertake
Not to exist, except as part of that one
Existence. We are thinking of happiness. In such case,
We must not count years. For happiness has no measurable pace.
Scarcely in consciousness, a hand finds, on stone, a hand.

They are in contact. Past lake, over mountain, last light
Probes for contact with the soft-shadowed land.

V

Old-Time Childhood in Kentucky

When I was a boy I saw the world I was in.
I saw it for what it was. Canebrakes with
Track beaten down by bear paw. Tobacco,
In endless rows, the pink inner flesh of black fingers
Crushing to green juice tobacco worms plucked
From a leaf. The great trout,
Motionless, poised in the shadow of his
Enormous creek-boulder.
But the past and the future broke on me, as I got older.

Strange, into the past I first grew. I handled the old bullet-mold.
I drew out a saber, touched an old bayonet, I dreamed
Of the death-scream. Old spurs I tried on.
The first great General Jackson had ridden just north to our state
To make a duel legal—or avoid the law.
It was all for honor. He said: "I would have killed him
Even with his hot lead in my heart." This for honor. I longed
To understand. I said the magic word.
I longed to say it aloud, to be heard.

I saw the strategy of Bryce's Crossroads, saw
The disposition of troops at Austerlitz, but knew
It was far away, long ago. I saw
The marks of the old man's stick in the dust, heard
The old voice explaining. His eyes weren't too good,
So I read him books he wanted. Read him
Breasted's *History of Egypt*. Saw years uncoil like a snake.
I built a pyramid with great care. There interred
Pharaoh's splendor and might.
Excavation next summer exposed that glory to man's sight.

At a cave mouth my uncle showed me crinoid stems,
And in limestone skeletons of the fishy form of some creature.
"All once under water," he said, "no saying the millions

Of years." He walked off, the old man still with me. "Grandpa,"
I said, "what do you do, things being like this?" "All you can,"
He said, looking off through treetops, skyward. "Love
Your wife, love your get, keep your word, and
If need arises die for what men die for. There aren't
Many choices.
And remember that truth doesn't always live in the number of voices."

He hobbled away. The woods seemed darker. I stood
In the encroachment of shadow. I shut
My eyes, head thrown back, eyelids black.
I stretched out the arm on each side, and, waterlike,
Wavered from knees and hips, feet yet firm-fixed, it seemed,
On shells, in mud, in sand, in stone, as though
In eons back I grew there in that submarine
Depth and lightlessness, waiting to discover
What I would be, might be, after ages—how many?—had rolled over.

Covered Bridge

Another land, another age, another self
Before all had happened that has happened since
And is now arranged on the shelf
Of memory in a sequence that I call Myself.

How can you think back and know
Who was the boy, sleepless, who lay
In a moonless night of summer, but with star-glow
Gemming the dewy miles, and acres, you used to go?

You think of starlight on the river, star
By star declaring its motionless, holy self,
Except at the riffle by the sandbar.
You wondered if reflection was seen by the sky's star.

Long, long ago, some miles away,
There was an old covered bridge across that stream,
And if impact of hoof or wheel made the loose boards sway,
That echo wandered the landscape, night or day.

But if by day, the human bumble and grind
Absorbed the sound, or even birdsong
Interfered in its fashion, and only at night might you find
That echo filling the vastness of your mind,

Till you wondered what night, long off, you would set hoof
On those loose boards and then proceed
To trot through the caverning dark beneath that roof.
Going where? Just going. That would be enough.

Then silence would wrap that starlit land,
And you would sleep—who now do not sleep
As you wonder why you cannot understand
What pike, highway, or path has led you from land to land,

*

From year to year, to lie in what strange room,
Where to prove identity you now lift up
Your own hand—scarcely visible in that gloom.

Re-interment: Recollection of a Grandfather

What a strange feeling all the years to carry
It in your head! Once—say almost
A hundred and sixty-odd years ago, and
Miles away—a young woman carried it
In her belly, and smiled. It was
Not lonely there. It did not see
Her smile, but knew itself part of the world
It lived in. Do you remember a place like that?

How strange now to feel it—that presence, lonely
But not alone, locked in my head.
Are those strange noises
All night in my skull
But fingers fumbling to get out?
He knows few others there or what they talk about.
More lonely than ever he must feel with the new, strange voices.

I hear in dream the insane colloquy and wrangling.
Is that his croak demanding explanation
Of the totally illegal seizure? Then tussle and tangling.
But whence the choked weeping, manic laughter, lips moving in prayer?
It's a mob scene of some sort, and then
Zip and whish, like bat wings in dark air,
That sometimes fill the great dome my shoulders bear.
But sometimes silence; and I seem to see
How out of the jail of my head he comes free.
And in twilight,
His lips move without sound, his hands stretch out to me there.
But his face fades from my sight.

Then sometimes I wake, and I know what will wake me.
It's again the fingernails clawing to get out,
To get out and tell me a thousand things to make me

Aware of what life's obligation is. Nails dig at a skull-seam.
They are stronger and sharper each year. Or is that a dream?
Each year more clawlike—as I watch hair go thin and pate gleam.
I strain to hear him speak, but words come too low
From that distance inside my skull,
And there's nothing to do but feel my heart full
Of what was true more than three-score years ago.

Some night, not far off, I'll sleep with no such recollection—
Not even his old-fashioned lingo and at dinner the ritual grace,
Or the scratched-in-dust map of Shiloh, and Bloody Pond,
Or the notion a man's word should equal his bond,
And the use of a word like *honor* as no comic disgrace.
And in our last communal trance, when the past has left no trace,
He'll not feel the world's contempt, or condescending smile,
For there'll be nobody left, in that after-while,
To love him—or recognize his kind. Certainly not his face.

Last Meeting

A Saturday night in August when
Farm folks and tenants and black farmhands
Used to crowd the street of a market town
To do their "traden," and chew the rag,

And to hide the likker from women hung out
Behind the poolroom or barbershop—
If you were white. If black, in an alley.
And the odor of whiskey mixed with the sweat

And cheap perfume, and high heels waggled
On worn bricks, and through the crowd
I saw her come. I see her now
As plain as then—some forty years back.

It's like a flash, and still she comes,
Comes peering at me, not sure yet,
For I'm in my city clothes and hat,
But in the same instant we recognize

Each other. I see the shrunken old woman
With bleary eyes and yellow-gray skin,
And walking now with the help of a stick.
We hug and kiss there in the street.

"Ro-Penn, Ro-Penn, my little tadpole,"
She said, and patted my cheek, and said,
"Git off yore hat so I'll see yore haid."
And I did. She ran her hands through thinning hair.

"Not fahr-red, like it used to be."
And ran her fingers some more. "And thinner,
And sandy color some places too."
Then she rocked her arms like cuddling a child,

*

51

And crooned, and said, "Now big and gone
Out in the wide world—but 'member me!"
I tried to say "I couldn't forget,"
But the words wouldn't come, and I felt how frail

Were the vertebrae I clasped. I felt
Tears run down beside her nose,
And a crazy voice, like some half-laugh,
Said, "Chile, yore Ma's dead, yore Pappy ole,

"But I'm hangen on fer what I'm wuth."
So we said goodbye, with eyes staring at us
And laughter in some corner, somewhere.
That was the last time we ever met.

All's changed. The faces on the street
Are changed. I'm rarely back. But once
I tried to find her grave, and failed.
Next time I'll promise adequate time.

And find it. I might take store-bought flowers
(Though not a florist in twenty miles),
But a fruit jar full of local zinnias
Might look even better with jimson weed.

It's nigh half a lifetime I haven't managed,
But there must be enough time left for that.

VI

Muted Music

As sultry as the cruising hum
Of a single fly lost in the barn's huge, black
Interior, on a Sunday afternoon, with all the sky
Ablaze outside—so sultry and humming
Is memory when in barn-shade, eyes shut,
You lie in hay, and wonder if that empty, lonely,
And muted music was all the past was, after all.
Does the past now cruise your empty skull like
That blundering buzz at barn-height—which is dark
Except for the window at one gable, where
Daylight is netted gray with cobwebs, and the web
Dotted and sagged with blunderers that once could cruise and hum.

What do you really know
Of that world of decision and
Action you once strove in? What
Of that world where now
Light roars, while you, here, lulled, lie
In a cunningly wrought and mathematical

Box of shade, and try, of all the past, to remember
Which was *what, what, which.* Perhaps
That sultry hum from the lone bumbler, cruising high
In shadow, is the only sound that truth can make,
And into that muted music you soon sink
To hear at last, at last, what you have strained for
All the long years, and sometimes at dream-verge thought

You heard—the song the moth sings, the babble
Of falling snowflakes (in a language
No school has taught you), the scream
Of the reddening bud of the oak tree

As the bud bursts into the world's brightness.

The Whole Question

You'll have to rethink the whole question. This
Getting born business is not as simple as it seemed,
Or midwife thought, or doctor deemed. It is,
Time shows, more complicated than either—or you—ever dreamed.

If it can be said that you dreamed anything
Before what's called a hand slapped blazing breath
Into you, snatched your dream's lulling nothing-
ness into what Paul called the body of this death.

You had not, for instance, previsioned the terrible thing called love,
Which began with a strange, sweet taste and bulbed softness while
Two orbs of tender light leaned there above.
Sometimes your face got twisted. They called it a smile.

You noticed how faces from outer vastness might twist, too.
But sometimes different twists, with names unknown,
And there were noises with no names you knew,
And times of dark silence when you seemed nothing—or gone.

Years passed, but sometimes seemed nothing except the same.
You knew more words, but they were words only, only—
Metaphysical midges that plunged at the single flame
That centered the infinite dark of your skull; or lonely,

You woke in the dark of real night to hear the breath
That seemed to promise reality in the vacuum
Of the sleepless dream beginning when underneath
The curtain dawn seeps, and on wet asphalt wet tires hum.

Yes, you must try to rethink what is real. Perhaps
It is only a matter of language that traps you. You
May yet find a new one in which experience overlaps
Words. Or find some words that make the Truth come true.

Old Photograph of the Future

That center of attention—an infantile face
That long years ago showed, no doubt, pink and white—
Now faded, and in the photograph only a trace
Of grays, not much expression in sight.

That center of attention, swathed in a sort of white dress,
Is precious to the woman who, pretty and young,
Leans with a look of surprised blessedness
At the mysterious miracle forth-sprung.

In the background somewhat, the masculine figure
Looms, face agleam with achievement and pride.
In black coat, derby at breast, he is quick to assure
You the world's in good hands—lay your worries aside.

The picture is badly faded. Why not?
Most things show wear around seventy-five,
And that's the age this picture has got.
The man and woman no longer, of course, live.

They lie side by side in whatever love survives
Under green turf, or snow, and that child, years later, stands there
While old landscapes blur and he in guilt grieves
Over nameless promises unkept, in undefinable despair.

Why Boy Came to Lonely Place

Limestone and cedar. Indigo shadow
On whiteness. The sky is flawlessly blue.
Only the cicada speaks. No bird. I do not know
Why I have these miles come. Here is only *I*. Not *You*.

Did I clamber these miles of distance
Only to quiver now in identity?
You are yourself only by luck, disaster, or chance,
And only alone may believe in your reality.

What drove you forth?—
Age thirteen, ignorant, lost in the world,
Canteen now dry and of what worth
With the cheese sandwich crumbling, and lettuce brown-curled?

Under the ragged shadow of cedar
You count the years you have been in the world,
And wonder what heed or
Care the world would have had of your absence as it whirled

In the iron groove of its circuit of space.
You say the name they gave you. That's all you are.
You move your fingers down your face,
And wonder how many years you'll be what you are.

But what is that? To find out you come to this lonely place.

Platonic Lassitude

Not one leaf stirs, though a high few,
As they hang without motion, shine translucently green
Against the depth of the sky's depthless blue.
The brook is shrunk. It meditates in serene

Silence. You see the warbler's throat palpitate
With heat. That is the only motion you see.
The mountain seems to float, to have no weight.
It may even sway, drift away into infinity,

Like a child's balloon at a circus. No fly, no gnat,
Stirs through the bright unreality of air.
Your lungs seem to have no function, and you have forgot
The substance breathed, and the *near* and the *far* where-

by you locate yourself, and the world
You're in, seem to lose distinction. No utterance
May come again, and the smoke that is curled
From a chimney may never uncurl in greater or lesser distance.

By brookside, by woodsedge, no bird sings or woodpecker taps,
And like the collage of a child to blue paper glued, the sun
Hangs, and you lie in the world's ontological collapse,
And ask if all is accomplished, all now done,

And even the past dissolves like a dream of mist,
Which is a new joy, that unlike the old, cannot end.
So, lulled, you loll in the lap of Time's wave, and the great crest,
With its tattered glory and gleam of foam-fringe, will never descend.

Or will it? To remind you
That nothing defines itself in joy or sorrow,
The crow calls from the black cliff forgotten but beckoning behind you.
Had you forgotten that history is only the fruit of tomorrow?

Seasons

I. DOWNWARDNESS

Under ledges of snow out-thrust from ledges
Of stone, once ledges of ice, water swells black,
With white whirlpools of sputum at edges.
At the edge of the forest I have seen the year's first bear track.

Downstream, a high out-thrust of snow groans, loses structure,
Falls in a smother and splash of white water boiling—
But not from heat. Boulders go grudging and grinding in rupture,
And one, heaved in air, chimes like a bell in that moiling.

After that tumult your ears with silence are tingling.
But, no, not silence. Your ears deceive.
Yes, listen! What seemed such silence is only the singing
Of a thousand driblets and streamlets that receive

Stored snow-waters, ice-waters, earth-waters, freed now in season
On the vast mountain, where they even explore
The most secret channel a root drills in its personal reason.
Here gravity is the only god, and water knows no more

Than the lust for downwardness, and the deepest coil.
But time will change, clouds again draw up buckets, day-
light glitter in the highest leaf like green foil,
And in earth-darkness moisture will climb the lattices of clay.

All night we now hear the desperate downwardness.
All day we have watched the last icicle
Drip, drop by drop, as though from a wound—grow less and less.
Dark comes again. Shut eyes, and think of a sacred cycle.

II. INTERLUDE OF SUMMER

Even in the spruce-dark gorge the last
Fringe of ice is in fatal deliquescence,
And rising waters heave to shoulder a boulder past.
Green will soon creep back in white's absence.

Each day, at mathematically accelerated pace,
The yet unseen sun will flood the eastern notch
With crimson, and you pick up a shoe, and yawn, and face
The morning news-screen of the world's hotchpotch or bloody botch.

Evening by evening, the climactic melodrama of
Day flares from behind the blackening silhouette
Of the mountain for the last and majestic pyre of
What of today you can remember, or forget.

Later and later each day, the eastern notch is now flooded
By dawn, and eyes gaze blankly at the world's disaster
With customary indifference, for you know fate is hooded.
The woodland violet that was your love is replaced by the roadside aster.

The faces of the children are now hardening toward definition.
Your own life seems to lose definition, as it did last year.
But garden and grape-arbor have fulfilled your ambition,
And gullet has sucked juice from the golden and tooth-gored pear.

An old friend dies this summer, and now whose carefully
Composed letters will challenge? But your own health is good.
Conversation
Turns to New England foliage, which has begun beautifully.
We might come back for a weekend of delightful observation.

After all, aesthetics is a branch of philosophy.

The Place

From shelving cliff-darkness, green arch and nave
Skyward aspire, translucently, to heights
Where tattered gold tags of sunlight twirl, swing,
Or downward sift to the upturned eye. Upward,
The eye probes infinite distance, infinite
Light, while foot, booted, tangled in fern,
Grips stone. Fern
Bleeds on stone.

       This
Is the hour of the unbounded loneliness. This
Is the hour of the self's uncertainty
Of self. This is the hour when
Prayer might be a possibility, if
It were. This
Is the hour when what is remembered is
Forgotten. When
What is forgotten is remembered, and
You are not certain which is which.
But tell me:

       How had you ever forgotten that spot
Where once wild azalea bloomed? And what there passed? And forgotten
That truth may lurk in irony? How,
Alone in a dark piazza, as the cathedral clock
Announced 3 A.M. to old tiles of the starless city, could you bear
To remember the impossible lie, told long before, elsewhere?
But a lie you had found all too possible.

Self is the cancellation of self, and now is the hour.
Self is the mutilation of official meanings, and this is the place.
You hear water of minor musical utterance
On stone, but from what direction?
You hear, distantly, a bird-call you cannot identify.

Is the shadow of the cliff creeping upon you?
You are afraid to look at your watch.

You think of the possibility of lying on stone,
Among fern fronds, and waiting
For the shadow to find you.
The stars would not be astonished
To catch a glimpse of the form through interstices
Of leaves now black as enameled tin. Nothing astounds the stars.
They have long lived. And you are not the first
To come to such a place seeking the most difficult knowledge.

First Moment of Autumn Recognized

Hills haven the last cloud. However white. From brightest blue
Spills glitter of afternoon, more champagne than ever
Summer. Bubble and sparkle burst in
Tang, taste, tangle, tingle, delicious
On tongue of spirit, joyful in eye-beam. We know
This to be no mere moment, however brief,
However blessèd, for
Moment means time, and this is no time,
Only the dream, untimed, between
Season and season. Let the leaf, gold, of birch,
Of beech, forever hang, not vegetable matter mortal, but
In no whatsoever breath of
Air. No—embedded in
Perfection of crystal, purer
Than air. You, embedded too in
Crystal, stand, your being perfected
At last, in the instant itself which is unbreathing.

Can you feel breath brush your damp
Lips? How can you know?

Paradigm of Seasons

Each year is like a snake that swallows its tail.
How long since we have learned, of seasons, the paradigm?
We know how cloud-scut and scud, north-bred, come scouting
The land out for winter, its waiting bulk. Come skirmishing, come scouting.
Then red leaf, gold leaf, then winter's choked road. Spring
Brings hope, even if we have
Ice-dam of river to flood the farmer's cellar. But
We know, too, how the heart, forgetting irony, stares at
The first apple bough to offer blossom,
Parody of snow. We know
The sweetness of the first secret
Tear, not brushed away. Summer
Is manic in strength, or lazy in maple shade and
Dry sweat. Summer dreams of glut. Summer slides
Over night-nakedness like a wave coming in with
The weight of moonlight like ocean beyond. But
On the rattle-trap iron of the slum fire-escape
At night you can see a match flare
To light a marijuana cigarette. And out of boredom
Two fingers penetrate a vagina.

                              Before long,
Of course, letters addressed to your familiar rural
Tin mailbox cease to arrive there. Now aging widows
In bifocals, with lower jaw slightly quivering, are
Carefully driven north from New York, in
Black sedans, with the price of gasoline no object.
They come to feed the spiritual part upon
The sight of New England foliage in splendor. Some
May even claim descent from Plymouth Rock,
And the saints thereof. Sometimes the chauffeur
Might have an equal claim, but doesn't know it.
But now the ladies are worrying about

Their houses in Florida. Soon,
From the mountains, you can hear the report
Of the authoritative rifle.

            Later,
Though you cannot hear it, there will be
The painful bellows of the lungs of an aging man
Who follows, with a burden of supplies on his back,
A snow-choked trail.

If Snakes Were Blue

If snakes were blue, it was the kind of day
That would uncoil in a luxurious ease
As each mica-bright scale exposed a flange of gold,
And slowly, slowly, the golden eyes blinked.

It was the kind of day that takes forever—
As though minutes, minutes, could never be counted—to slide
Among the clouds like pink lily-pads floating
In a crystal liquid pure enough to drink.

And there was no distinction now between
Light and shadow except the mystic and faint
Sense of adaptation of the iris,
As light diminished and the first star shone,

And the last veery, hidden in a thicket of alder,
Thought it would break its heart perhaps—or yours.
Let it be yours, then. For such gentle breaking
In that ambiguous moment could not be

Less than a blessing, or the kind of promise
We give ourselves in childhood when first dawn
Makes curtains go gold, and all night's dreams flood back.
They had guaranteed our happiness forever.

And in a way such promises may come true
In spite of all our evil days and ways.
True, few fulfillments—but look! In the distance lift peaks
Of glittering white above the wrath-torn land.

Little Girl Wakes Early

Remember when you were the first one awake, the first
To stir in the dawn-curdled house, with little bare feet
Cold on boards, every door shut and accurst,
And behind shut doors no breath perhaps drew, no heart beat.

You held your breath and thought how all over town
Houses had doors shut, and no whisper of breath sleeping,
And that meant no swinging, nobody to pump up and down,
No hide-and-go-seek, no serious play at housekeeping.

So you ran outdoors, bare feet from the dew wet,
And climbed the fence to the house of your dearest friend,
And opened your lips and twisted your tongue, all set
To call her name—but the sound wouldn't come in the end,

For you thought how awful, if there was no breath there
For answer. Tears start, you run home, where now mother,
Over the stove, is humming some favorite air.
You seize her around the legs, but tears aren't over,

And won't get over, not even when she shakes you—
And shakes you hard—and more when you can't explain.
Your mother's long dead. And you've learned that when loneliness
                                                          takes you
There's nobody ever to explain to—though you try again and again.

Winter Wheat: Oklahoma

The omelet of sunset vibrates in the great flat pan.
A certain amount of golden grease will spatter.
In distance the tractor is red, but without pride of
The glitter and brightness, with ink scarcely dry on the contract.
But still it makes black earth blacker when it treads with steel heels.

There's a half-mile to tread before it reaches the spot where
The old car waits. The omelet is long done before
The tractor's last blue-gray puff is puffed, and the cranky
Old bones of the driver, in denim swathed, creak down
From the seat of power. Aboard car, he slowly props

Head back, shuts eyes. When they open first stars are out,
Though pale. He hates to go home. It's rough to the lane,
And tough on sciatica. The lane ain't no broadway, nohow.
In the end, there's the tight rectangle of the little lawn-patch, two maples.
He sees the barn, the woodlot, the years. All his,

And his sweat's. The maples are big now. But she's not sitting
To wave when he gets close. Now no smoke in the chimney,
These nights. Well, just grab something, whatever. Then coffee.
A time it was booze. But booze made him wonder
How flesh would peel off cheekbones in earth out yonder, and if

All that gold he'd been so proud to pay good cash for,
For her poor teeth, now gleamed like light in that darkness.
Anyway, a man oughtn't sit and see tears ruin his booze.
He sits alone. Him not one for talking.
His boy writes every Christmas, will sure come next year.

*

That boy was his boy. Not begrudging sweat. But who
Could be sure about God taking care of His business? Wheat in,
And maybe He'd go skylarkin' off this time,
Like He does sometimes to pleasure Himself,
Whatever He does. And lets

A man's honest sweat just go for nothing.

VII

Youthful Picnic Long Ago: Sad Ballad on Box

In Tennessee once the campfire glowed
With steady joy in its semi-globe
Defined by the high-arched nave of oaks against
Light-years of stars and the
Last scream space makes beyond space. Faces,

In grave bemusement, leaned, eyes fixed
On the fingers white in their delicate dance
On the strings of the box. And delicate
Was the melancholy that swelled each heart, and timed
The pulse in wrist, and wrist, and wrist—all while
The face leaned over the box
In shadow of hair that in fire-light down-gleamed,
Smoother than varnish, and black. And like
A silver vine that upward to darkness twines,
The voice confirmed the sweet sadness
Young hearts gave us no right to.

No right to, yet. Though some day would,
As Time unveiled,
In its own dancing parody of grace,
The bony essence of each joke on joke.

But even back then perhaps we knew
That the dancing fingers enacted
A truth far past the pain declared
By that voice that somehow made pain sweet.

Would it be better or worse, if now
I could name the names I've lost, and see,
Virile or beautiful, those who, entranced, leaned.
I wish I knew what wisdom they had there learned.

*

The singer—her name, it flees the fastest!
If only she'd toss back that varnished black screen
Of beautiful hair, and let
Flame reveal the grave cheek-curve, eye-shine,
Then I'd know that much.
If not her name.

Even now.

History During Nocturnal Snowfall

Dark in the cubicle boxed from snow-darkness of night,
Where that soundless paradox summarizes the world,
We lie, each alone, and I reach a finger laid light
To a wrist that does not move, as I think of a body curled—

Is it an inch, or a world, away—a watch-tick
Or a century off? In darkness I compress my eyes
And wonder if I might devise the clever trick
Of making heartbeat with heartbeat synchronize.

Each has come a long way to this wordless and windless burrow,
Each, like a mole, clawing blindly, year after year,
Each clawing and clawing through blindness of joy and sorrow,
And neither knowing how the world outside might appear.

Could one guess the other's buried narrative?
How the other, in weal or woe, might have found
White darkness where, a finger on wrist, one might live
In the synchronized rhythm of heart, and heart, with no sound?

Was it a matter of chance? Or miracle?
Or which is which—for logic laughs at both?
Could it matter less as whiteness and darkness blending fall
And my finger touches a pulse to intuit its truth.

Whistle of the 3 A.M.

At 3 A.M., if the schedule held,
The express blew for the crossing a mile
Out of town, and you woke, and your heart swelled
With the thought that some night in your own dark cubicle,

You would whirl, in sleep or in contempt,
Past some straggle of town with scarcely a streetlight
To show the pale ghost, unloved, unkempt,
Of a place that would shuffle to life with the creak of daylight.

And once at that whistle you from bed crept,
Lifted curtains and wiped the frost from the pane,
And the magisterial headlight swept
Hills snow-white, white woods, white fields, until again

There was nothing but marmoreal moonlight
Defining the structure of night—and your feet
Cold on boards. Did you stare at the sheet's trancelike white-
ness, which held no hint of the world's far fury and heat?

Times change, man changes, and thirty-five thousand
Feet down, what whistle wakes any boy
To the world's bliss and rage, and the raging sand
Of the sandblast of History? Am I the boy

Who last remembers the 3 A.M.?
What if some hold real estate nearby,
A good six feet long, but not one of them
Would wake, I guess, to listen, and wonder why

The schedule's gone dead of the 3 A.M.

Last Night Train

In that slick and new-fangled coach we go slam-banging
On rackety ruin of a roadbed, past caterpillar-
Green flash of last light on deserted platforms,
And I watch the other passenger at this
Late hour—a hundred and eighty pounds of
Flesh, black, female, middle-aged,
Unconsciously flung by roadbed jerks to wallow,
Unshaped, unhinged, in
A purple dress. Straps of white sandals
Are loosened to ease the bulge of color-contrasting bare instep.
Knees wide, the feet lie sidewise, sole toward sole. They
Have walked so far. Head back, flesh snores.
I wonder what she has been doing all day in N.Y.

My station at last. I look back once.
Is she missing hers? I hesitate to ask, and the snore
Is suddenly snatched into eternity.

The last red light fades into distance and darkness like
A wandering star. Where that brief roar just now was,
A last cricket is audible. That lost
Sound makes me think, with quickly suppressed
Nostalgia, of
A country lane, late night, late autumn—and there,
Alone, again I stand, part of all.
Alone, I now stand under the green station light,
Part of nothing but years.

I stare skyward at uncountable years beyond
My own little aura of pale-green light—
The complex of stars is steady in its operation.
Smell of salt sedge drifts in from seaward,
And I think of swimming, naked and seaward,
In starlight forever.

*

73

But I look up the track toward Bridgeport. I feel
Like blessing the unconscious wallow of flesh-heap
And white sandals unstrapped at bulging of instep.

I hear my heels crunch on gravel, making
My way to a parked car.

74

VIII

Milton: A Sonnet

No doubt he could remember how in the past
Late carmine had bathed the horizon with its wide kindness.
Not now. In darkness he prayed, and at the last
Moved through the faithful brilliance they called blindness,
Knew burgeoning Space in which old space hummed like a fly,
And Time that devoured itself to defecate
A nobler dimension of that self whereby
The past and future are intrinsicate
To form a present in which the blessèd heart
May leap like a gleaming fish from water into
Sunlight before the joy-flashed curve may dart
Back to the medium of deep wisdom through
A pavane of bubbles like pearls, again to slash
Upward, and upward again, and, in joy, flash.

Whatever You Now Are

In the depth and rustle of midnight, how do you know
What is the dream and who the dreamer? Oh yes,
You fell asleep to the star-bit and murmurous flow
Of the stream beneath your window, but frontierless
Are the stream and the Self conjunct all night long.
How is the difference defined between singer and song?

Is it you that flows from distance, to distance,
With the tune of time and blood intertwined forever?
Or does the dark stream of log-ripple and stone-chance
Define the pattern of your whole life's endeavor?
What elements, shadowy, in that dream interlace
In a region past categories of Time and Space?

Yes, think of the pale transparencies that lave
Stone, riffle, algae, and the moon-bright sandbar,
While music drifts to your shadowy cave
Of consciousness, whoever you now are—
But dawn breaks soon, and that self will have fled away.
Will a more strange one yet inhabit the precinct of day?

Wind and Gibbon

All night, over roof, over forest, you hear
Wind snore, shift, stir, like a dog uncomfortable
In sleep, or dreaming. You think of leg
Twitching. Paw jerking. Claw
Unconsciously scraping the wood floor. You drowse.
Wake. Decide it is only a spruce bough wind-dragging
Across the corner of the house, like a saw. Wind,
Suddenly, stops. Shifts. Again lifts. Has no mind
That could rationally dictate change. Its head
Is like a dried gourd rattling
A few dried seeds within. The wind
Is like a dream of History. Blows where it listeth.

You get up. Wander. Gibbon, you see,
Is on the shelf, volume by volume, solid as masonry. At random,
You seize one. It will be more comforting
Than the morning paper. The paper
Will gabble like paranoia, chitter in a strange tongue like
A capuchin, the organ-grinder's monkey.
You chunk up the fire. You do not hear the wind.

It does not matter where you begin. This is History.
Pick up any volume. Gibbon's hot lava
Seethes over the conical brim of the world whence
Lifts flame-tongue. Glowing,
It flows, like incandescent irony, over
Vineyard, sheepfold (but quickly soothes that
Frizzly tumult), stone hut, villa, the brawny and noble
Cockmaster about to insert the tool of wizardy, that
Moan-maker. It spills
Over empires, imperial palaces, the Crusader
Whose mount is hock-bloody. *In hoc signo.*

History is not truth. Truth is in the telling.

*

77

The lava flows on. Before dawn, you sleep. This, in your chair.

Long back the wind has stopped. The world is now white.
You face west. The mountain is white with snow.
From the new sun, back of your house, and thus
Invisible to you, a single
Beam, sky-arrowing, strikes
The mountain to dazzlement.

Delusion? — No!

In atmosphere almost too heavenly
Pure for nourishment of earthbound
Bone, or bone-borne flesh, I stood,
At last past sweat and swink, at crag-edge. Felt
My head swell like the sky that knew
No distance, and knew no sensation but blueness.

In that divine osmosis I stood
And felt each discrete and distinct stroke
Of the heart as it downward fled—
Cliff, cleft, gorge, chasm, and, far off,
Ravine cut in the flattening but still high glitter
Of earth. I saw afar the peek-a-boo of some stream's gleam.

Mind plays strange tricks on us.
One moment I felt the momentous, muscular thrust
Skyward of peak, then the thumb-and-forefinger twist
Of range on range. I entered in.
Was part of all. I knew the
Glorious light of inner darkness burn
Like the fundamental discovery.

Yes, stretch forth your arms like wings, and from your high stance,
Hawk-eyed, ride forth upon the emptiness of air, survey
Each regal contortion
And tortuous imagination of rock, wind, water, and know
Your own the power creating all.

Delusion? — No! For Truth has many moments.

Open your eyes. Who knows? This may be one.

Question at Cliff-Thrust

From the outthrust ledge of sea-cliff you
Survey, downward, the lazy tangle and untangle of
Foam fringe, not on sand, but sucking through
Age-rotten pumice and lava like old fruitcake lost in an angle of
A kitchen closet, the fruit long since nibbled away
By mouse-tooth. This is a day
Of merciless sun, no wind, and
Of distance, slick as oil, sliding infinitely away
To no far smudge of land.
You stare down at your cove beneath.
No blackness of rock shows,
Only the gradual darkening green as depth grows.
In that depth how far would breath
Hold? Down through gull-torn air
You lean forward and stare
At the shelving green of hypnosis.

Who would guess
It would be as easy as this?

A pebble companions your white downward flash.
You do not hear what must be its tiny splash
As, bladelike, your fingertips
Into the green surface slash
And your body, frictionless, slips
Into a green atmosphere,
Where you can hear
Only the nothingness of sound, and see
Only the one great green and unforgiving eye of depth that steadily
Absorbs your being in its intensity.
You take the downward strokes, some two or three.
Suddenly your lungs, aflame, burn.
But there is the beckoning downwardness
That you must fight before you turn, and in the turn

Begin the long climb toward lighter green, and light,
Until you lie in lassitude and strengthlessness
On the green bulge of ocean under the sight
Of one gull that screams from east to west and is

Demanding what?

It Is Not Dead

It is not dead. It is simply weighty with wisdom.
A long way and painful, it has come to become
What it is. In nameless heat under
Nameless pressure, liquefied,
It has tried
To find its true nature, seething in depth and darkness when earth
Was not yet ready to be torn asunder,
But heaved in silence, like throttled thunder.

What eons remained still
To await what cataclysmic birth
That exploded, roared, glowed
To change its liquid mind to hardness like glass, to iron will?
What name had the plowshare that plowed
It wide to the fury of light on a high place?
What determination interminable,
What years, did the crowbar of ice take
To pry from the crag-face
That mass to make
A scythe to reduce some undefined forest to splinters? Then the might
Of the first unmerciful grasp of the glacier, the grind,
The trundling descent in darkness, white
But absolute. What timeless thoughts ground in its downward mind?
Then fingers of water, weak but uncontrollable,
Worked in their tangle of multitudinous will,
Age after age, until
Half in, half out, of my brook it lies,
Honed to perfection, perfect in structure, moss-idle, sunlit.
And, naked, I lie on it,
Brooding on our common destinies.
Against the declaration of sunlight I close my eyes.

*

All night, it will lie there under the stars,
Attent to the riffle, and I lie, in brotherhood, where I lie,
Hearing the riffle too, though a curtain bars
Me in darkness except in one twisted spot where I spy
A fleeting fracture of the immensity of the night sky.

Sunset

Clouds clamber, turgid, the mountain, peakward
And pine-pierced, toward the
Vulgar and flaming apocalypse of day,
In which our errors are consumed
Like fire in a lint-house—
Not repetitious
But different each day, for day to day nothing
Is identical to eye or soul.
At night, at a late hour, I
Have asked stars the name of my soul.

"Oh, what shall I call my soul in a dire hour?"
But there is no answer from
Heavenly algebra, and you are left with
The implacable gaggles and military squadrons
Of ignorance, which have no
Originality and know
Nothing but repetition, and which
We call constellations.

Who knows his own name at the last?
How shall he speak to a soul that has none?
"Tell me that name," I cried, "that I may speak
In a dire hour." The dire hour
Is the time when you must speak
To your naked self—never
Before seen, nor known.

IX

Myth of Mountain Sunrise

Prodigious, prodigal, crags steel-ringing
To dream-hoofs nightlong, proverbial
Words stone-incised in language unknowable, but somehow singing
Their wisdom-song against disaster of granite and all
Moonless non-redemption on the left hand of dawn:
The mountain dimly wakes, stretches itself on windlessness. Feels its
                                    deepest chasm, waking, yawn.

The curdling agony of interred dark strives dayward, in stone
                                              strives though
No light here enters, has ever entered but
In ageless age of primal flame. But look! All mountains want slow-
ly to bulge outward extremely. The leaf, whetted on light, will cut
Air like butter. Leaf cries: "I feel my deepest filament in dark rejoice.
I know that the density of basalt has a voice."

How soon will the spiderweb, dew-dappled, gleam
In Pompeian glory! Think of a girl-shape, birch-white sapling, rising now
From ankle-deep brook-stones, head back-flung, eyes closed in first beam,
While hair—long, water-roped, past curve, coign, sway that no
                                              geometries know—
Spreads end-thin, to define fruit-swell of haunches, tingle of hand-hold.
The sun blazes over the peak. That will be the old tale told.

85

From

RUMOR
VERIFIED

Poems 1979-1980

To Peter and Ebie Blume

. . . i' vidi de le cose belle
che porta 'l ciel, per un pertugio tondo.
E quindi uscimmo a riveder le stelle.

—Dante: *Inferno*, Canto XXXIV
Edited by Charles S. Singleton

Chthonian Revelation: A Myth

Long before sun had toward the mountain dipped,
There downward at crag-fall, bare-footed, bare-hided but for
Beach-decency's minimum, they
Painfully picked past lava, past pumice, past boulders
High-hung and precarious over the sea-edge, awaiting
Last gust or earth-tremor. Below,
Lay the sand-patch, white
As the lace-fringe that, languid and lazy,
Teased from the edge of the sun-singing sea.

Few know what is there:
Sea and sand finger back into cave-shade where
Gothic, great strata,
Once torn in the shudder of earth and earth-agony, had
Down-reached to find footing in depth. Now deep
In arched dusk from the secret strand, the eye
Stares from that mystic and chthonian privacy
To far waters whose tirelessly eye-slashing blue
Commands the wide world beyond that secret purlieu.

After sun, how dark! Or after sun-scimitar, how
Gentle the touch of the shade's hypothetical hand. Farther on,
Farther in!—and on the soft sand he is sure
Of the track. Then looks back
Just once through the dwindling aperture
To the world of light-tangled detail
Where once life was led that now seems illusion of life
And swings in the distance with no more identity than
A dream half-remembered. He turns. His face lifts
To the soaring and scarcely definable nave,
From which darkness downward and endlessly sifts.

Eyes lower: and there,
In that drizzle of earth's inner darkness, she

Stands, face upward, arms up as in prayer or
Communion with whispers that wordlessly breathe—
There in columnar gracility stands, breasts,
In that posture, high. Eyes closed. And in
Such world of shadows, she,
From the light of her own inner being, glows.

Slowly, the lifted arms descend, fingers out,
Slightly parted. His eyes find the light of her eyes,
And over immeasurable distance,
Hands out, as though feeling his way in the act,
On the soundless sand he moves in his naked trance.
At last, fingertips make contact.

When in hermetic wisdom they wake, the cave-mouth is dim.
Once out, they find sun sinking under the mountain-rim,
And a last gleam boldly probes
High eastward the lone upper cloud. Scraps of nylon
Slip on like new skin, though cold, and feet
Find the rustle and kitten-tongue kiss of the foam creeping in.

A kilometer toward the headland, then home: they wade out,
And plunge. All wordless, this—
In a world where all words would be
Without meaning, and all they long to hear
Is the gull's high cry
Of mercilessly joyful veracity
To fill the hollow sky.

Side by side, stroke by stroke, in a fading light they move.
The sea pours over each stroke's frail groove.
Blackly, the headland looms. The first star is declared.
It is white above the mountain mass.
Eyes starward fixed, they feel the sea's long swell
And the darkling drag of nameless depth below.
They turn the headland, with starlight the only light they now know.
At arch-height of every stroke, at each fingertip, hangs
One drop, and the drops—one by one—are
About to fall, each a perfect universe defined
By its single, minuscule, radiant, enshrinèd star.

Looking Northward, Aegeanward: Nestlings on Seacliff

Chalky, steel-hard, or glass-slick, the cliff
That you crawl up, inch up, or clamber, till now,
Arms outspread, you cling to rotting scrub roots, and at last
See what you'd risked neck to see, the nub
Of rock-shelf outthrust from the shaded recess where,
From huddle of trash, dried droppings, and eggshell, lifts
The unfeathered pitiless weakness of necks that scarcely uphold
The pink corolla of beak-gape, the blind yearning lifeward.

In sun-blast, around and above, weave
The outraged screams that would net your head,
And wings slash the air with gleaming mercilessness,
While for toehold, or handhold, downward you grope,
Or for purchase to pause on and turn to the sun-crinkled sea,
To watch it fade northward into the
Horizon's blue ambiguity. You think
How long ago galleys—slim, black, bronze-flashing—bore
Northward too, and toward that quarter's blue dazzle of distance.
Or of a tale told.

And then think how, lost in the dimness of aeons, sea sloshed
Like suds in a washing machine, land heaved, and sky
At noon darkened, and darkness, not like any metaphor, fell,
And in that black fog gulls screamed as the feathers of gull-wing
From white flash to flame burst. That was the hour
When rooftree or keystone of palaces fell, and

Priest's grip drew backward the curls of the king's son until
Throat-softness was tightened, and the last cry
Was lost in the gargle of blood on bronze blade. The king,
In his mantle, had buried his face. But even
That last sacrifice availed naught. Ashes
Would bury all. Cities beneath sea sank.

*

In some stony, high field, somewhere, eyes,
Unbelieving, opened. They saw first,
The sky. Stared long. How little
They understood. But, slowly, began,
In new ignorance, the nature of Time.

You think of necks, unfeathered and feeble, upholding
The pink corolla of beak-gape—that blind yearning lifeward.

Going West

Westward the Great Plains are lifting, as you
Can tell from the slight additional pressure
The accelerator requires. The sun,
Man to man, stares you straight in the eye, and the
Ribbon of road, white, into the sun's eye
Unspools. Wheat stubble long behind,
Now nothing but range land. But,
With tire song lulling like love, gaze riding white ribbon, forward
You plunge. Blur of burnt goldness
Past eye-edge on each
Side back-whirling, you arrow
Into the heart of hypnosis.

This is one way to write the history of America.

It was that way that day—oh, long
Ago. I had to slap
The back of my neck to stay awake,
Eyes westward in challenge to sun-gaze, lids
Slitted for sight. The land,
Beyond miles of distance, fled
Backward to whatever had been,
As though Space were Time.
Now do I see the first blue shadow of foothills?
Or is that a cloud line?
When will snow, like a vision, lift there?

I do not see, sudden out of
A scrub clump, the wing-burst. See only
The bloody explosion, right in my face,
On the windshield, the sun and
The whole land forward, forever,
All washed in blood, in feathers, in gut-scrawl.

*

It is, of course, a fool pheasant.

Hands clamping the wheel with a death grip
To hold straight while brakes scream, I,
With no breath, at the blood stare. The ditch
Is shallow enough when the car, in the end, rolls in.

Clumps of old grass, old newspaper, dry dirt—
All this got the worst off. Slowly,
Red sunset now reddening to blood streaks,
Westward the car moved on. Blood
Fried on the glass yet stove-hot. For the day,
It had sure been a scorcher. Later,
Handfuls of dry dirt would scrape off the fried blood.
Eventually, water at a gas station.

Even now, long afterwards, the dream.

I have seen blood explode, blotting out sun, blotting
Out land, white ribbon of road, the imagined
Vision of snowcaps, white in their purity.

Rumor Verified

Since the rumor has been verified, you can, at least,
Disappear. You will no longer be seen at the Opera,
With your head bowed studiously, to one side a little,
Nor at your unadvertised and very exclusive
Restaurant, discussing wine with the sommelier,
Nor at your club, setting modestly forth your subtle opinion.

Since the rumor has been verified, you can try, as in dream,
To have lived another life—not with the father
Of rigid self-discipline, and x-ray glance,
Not with the mother, overindulgent and pretty,
Who toyed with your golden locks, slipped money on the side,
And waved a witch's wand for success, and a rich marriage.

Since the rumor has been verified, you may secretly sneak
Into El Salvador, or some such anguished spot,
Of which you speak the language, dreaming, trying to believe
That, orphaned, you grew up in poverty and vision, struggling
For learning, for mankind's sake. Here you pray with the sick, kiss lepers.

Since the rumor has been verified, you yearn to hold
A cup of cold water for the dying man to sip.
You yearn to look deep into his eyes and learn wisdom.
Or perhaps you have a practical streak and seek
Strange and derelict friends, and for justification lead
A ragtag squad to ambush the uniformed patrol.

Well, assuming the rumor verified—that may be
The only logical course: at any price,
Even bloodshed, however ruthless, to change any dominant order
And the secret corruption of power that makes us what we seem.
Yes, what is such verification against a strength of will?

*

But even in the face of the rumor, you sometimes shudder,
Seeing men as old as you who survive the terror
Of knowledge. You watch them slyly. What is their trick?
Do they wear a Halloween face? But what can you do?
Perhaps pray to God for strength to face the verification
That you are simply a man, with a man's dead reckoning, nothing more.

Mountain Mystery

On the mountain trail, all afternoon,
Gravel, uncertain, grinds under hoof.
On left side, with scrub growth, the cliff hangs.
On right, hypnotic emptiness.

Far down, in distance, a stream uncoils,
Like nothing more than a glittering wire
Tangled in stone-slots, lost on the plain,
In distance dissolved, or down canyon, gone.

You stop. You turn and know what already
You know: snow commanding west ranges, sun
Yet high. Again, eastward turn, and the sun's
Hot hand, fingers spread, is pressed against your shoulders.

Soaring in sunlight, eastward, the eagle
Swings to a height invisible
Except when light catches a bright flash of wing.
You open your lips in infinite thirst for

The altitude's wine. All, all of the past
Is gone. Yet what is the past but delusion?
Or future? In timeless light the world swims.
Alone, alone, you move through the timeless

Light. Toward what? The ranch in the valley,
Some ten miles away—what but delusion?
Alone, but not alone, for if
You lift your eyes, you see, some forty

Feet off, her there—unless, of course,
The track now rounds an abutment, and she
Has ceased to exist, and you are alone
In the world's metaphysical beauty of light.

*

Only alone do you then think of love.
Eyes shut, you think how, in saddle, that narrow
Waist sways. You think how, when soon the trail straightens,
She will lean back to smile. Her eyes will be bright.

You pass the abutment. Beyond, the great mesa
Sinks blue. The world falls away, falls forever.
But she sways in the saddle, turns, smiles, and your heart
Leaps up. Then cries out: *Oh, what is enough?*

That night you will lie in your bed, not alone—
But alone. In dark paradox, you lie
And think of the screaming gleam of the world
In which you have passed alone, lost—

And in dark, lost, lain, hearing frailty of breath beside.

Vermont Ballad: Change of Season

All day the fitful rain
Had wrought new traceries,
New quirks, new love-knots, down the pane.

And what do I see beyond
That fluctuating gray
But a world that seems to be God-abandoned—

Last leaf, rain-soaked, from my high
Birch falling, the spruce wrapped in thought,
And the mountain dissolving rain-gray to gray sky.

In the gorge, like a maniac
In sleep, the stream grinds its teeth,
As I lay a new log at the fireplace-back.

It is not that I am cold:
But that I think how the flux,
Three quarters now of a century old,

Has faithfully swollen and ebbed,
In life's brilliantly flashing red
Through all flesh, in vein and artery webbed.

But now it feels viscous and gray
As I watch the gray of the world,
And that thought seems soaked in my brain to stay.

But who is master here?
The turn of the season, or I?
What lies in the turn of the season to fear?

*

If I set muzzle to forehead
And pull the trigger, I'll see
The world in a last flood of vital red—

Not gray—that cataracts down.
No, I go to the windowpane
That rain's blurring tracery claims as its own,

And stare up the mountain track
Till I see in the rain-dusk, trudging
With stolid stride, his bundle on back,

A man with no name, in the gloom,
On an errand I cannot guess.
No sportsman—no! Just a man in his doom.

In this section such a man is not an uncommon sight.
In rain or snow, you pass, and he says: "Kinda rough tonight."

Dead Horse in Field

In the last, far field, half-buried
In barberry bushes red-fruited, the thoroughbred
Lies dead, left foreleg shattered below knee,
A .30-30 in heart. In distance,
I now see gorged crows rise ragged in wind. The day
After death I had gone for farewell, and the eyes
Were already gone—that
The beneficent work of crows. Eyes gone,
The two-year-old could, of course, more readily see
Down the track of pure and eternal darkness.

A week later I couldn't get close. The sweet stink
Had begun. That damned wagon mudhole
Hidden by leaves as we galloped—I found it.
Spat on it. As a child would. Next day
The buzzards. How beautiful in air!—carving
The slow, concentric, downward pattern of vortex, wing-glint
On wing-glint. From the house,
Now with glasses, I see
The squabble and pushing, the waggle of wattle-red heads.

At evening I watch the buzzards, the crows,
Arise. They swing black in nature's flow and perfection,
High in sad carmine of sunset. Forgiveness
Is not indicated. It is superflous. They are
What they are.

How long before I go back to see
That intricate piece of
Modern sculpture, white now,
Assuming in stasis
New beauty! Then,
A year later, I'll see
The green twine of vine, each leaf

Heart-shaped, soft as velvet, beginning
Its benediction.

It thinks it is God.

Can you think of some ground on which that may be gainsaid?

The Corner of the Eye

The poem is just beyond the corner of the eye.
You cannot see it—not yet—but sense the faint gleam,

Or stir. It may be like a poor little shivering fieldmouse,
One tiny paw lifted from snow while, far off, the owl

Utters. Or like breakers, far off, almost as soundless as dream.
Or the rhythmic rasp of your father's last breath, harsh

As the grind of a great file the blacksmith sets to hoof.
Or the whispering slither the torn morning newspaper makes,

Blown down an empty slum street in New York, at midnight,
Past dog shit and garbage cans, while the full moon,

Phthisic and wan, above the East River, presides
Over that last fragment of history which is

Our lives. Or the foggy glint of old eyes of
The sleepless patient who no longer wonders

If he will once more see in that window the dun-
Bleached dawn that promises what. Or the street corner

Where always, for years, in passing you felt, unexplained, a pang
Of despair, like nausea, till one night, late, late on that spot

You were struck stock-still and again remembered—felt
Her head thrust to your shoulder, she clinging, while you

Mechanically pat the fur coat, hear sobs, and stare up
Where tall buildings, frailer than reed-stalks, reel among stars.

*

Yes, something there at eye-edge lurks, hears ball creak in socket,
Knows, before you do, tension of muscle, change

Of blood pressure, heart-heave of sadness, foot's falter, for
It has stalked you all day, or years, breath rarely heard, fangs dripping.

And now, any moment, great hindquarters may hunch, ready—
Or is it merely a poem, after all?

What Voice at Moth-Hour

What voice at moth-hour did I hear calling
As I stood in the orchard while the white
Petals of apple blossoms were falling,
Whiter than moth-wing in that twilight?

What voice did I hear as I stood by the stream,
Bemused in the murmurous wisdom there uttered,
While ripples at stone, in their steely gleam,
Caught last light before it was shuttered?

What voice did I hear as I wandered alone
In a premature night of cedar, beech, oak,
Each foot set soft, then still as stone
Standing to wait while the first owl spoke?

The voice that I heard once at dew-fall, I now
Can hear by a simple trick. If I close
My eyes, in that dusk I again know
The feel of damp grass between bare toes,

Can see the last zigzag, sky-skittering, high,
Of a bullbat, and even hear, far off, from
Swamp-cover, the whip-o-will, and as I
Once heard, hear the voice: *It's late! Come home.*

Another Dimension

Over meadows of Brittany, the lark
Flames sunward, divulging, in tinseled fragments from
That height, song. Song is lost
In the blue depth of sky, but
We know it is there at an altitude where only
God's ear may hear.

Dividing fields, long hedges, in white
Bloom powdered, gently slope to the
Blue of sea that glitters in joy of its being.

Once I lay on the grass and looked upward
To feel myself redeemed into
That world which had no meaning but itself,
As I, lying there, had only the present, no future or past.

Yes—who was the man who on the midnight street corner,
Alone, once stood, while sea-fog
Put out last lights, electric or heavenly?
Who knows that history is the other name for death?
Who, from the sweated pillow, wakes to know
How truth can lie? Who knows that jealousy,
Like a chinch-bug under the greenest turf, thrives?
Who learned that kindness can be the last cruelty?

I have shut my eyes and seen the lark flare upward.
All was as real as when my eyes were open.
I have felt earth breathe beneath my shoulder blades.
I have strained to hear, sun-high, that Platonic song.

It may be that some men, dying, have heard it.

English Cocker: Old and Blind

With what painful deliberation he comes down the stair,
At the edge of each step one paw suspended in air,
And distrust. Does he thus stand on a final edge
Of the world? Sometimes he stands thus, and will not budge,

With a choking soft whimper, while monstrous blackness is whirled
Inside his head, and outside too, the world
Whirling in blind vertigo. But if your hand
Merely touches his head, old faith comes flooding back—and

The paw descends. His trust is infinite
In you, who are, in his eternal night,
Only a frail scent subject to the whim
Of wind, or only a hand held close to him

With a dog biscuit, or, in a sudden burst
Of temper, the force that jerks that goddamned, accurst
Little brute off your bed. But remember how you last saw
Him hesitate in his whirling dark, one paw

Suspended above the abyss at the edge of the stair,
And remember that musical whimper, and how, then aware
Of a sudden sweet heart-stab, you knew in him
The kinship of all flesh defined by a halting paradigm.

Have You Ever Eaten Stars?

(A Note on Mycology)

Scene: A glade on a bench of the mountain,
Where beech, birch, and spruce meet
In peace, though in peace not intermingled,
Around the slight hollow, upholstered
In woods-earth damp, and soft, centuries old—
Spruce needle, beech leaf, birch leaf, ground-pine
                                  belly-crawling,
And fern frond, and deadfall of birch, grass blade
So biblically frail, and sparse in that precinct where
The sunray makes only its brief
And perfunctory noontide visitation.
All, all in that cycle's beneficence
Of being are slowly absorbed—oh, slowly—into
What once had fed them. And now,
In silence as absolute as death,
Or as vision in breathlessness,
Your foot may come. Or mine,
As when I, sweat-soaked in summer's savagery,
Might here come, and stand
In that damp cool, and peace of process,
And hear, somewhere, a summer-thinned brook descending,
Past stone, and stone, its musical stair.

But late, once in the season's lateness, I,
After drouth had broken, rain come and gone,
And sky been washed to a blue more delicate,
Came. Stood. Stared. For now,
Earth, black as a midnight sky,
Was, like sky-darkness, studded with
Gold stars, as though
In emulation, however brief.
There, by a deer trail, by deer dung nourished,
Burst the gleam, rain-summoned,

Of bright golden chanterelles.
However briefly, however small and restricted, here was
A glade-burst of glory.

Later, I gathered stars into a basket.

Question: What can you do with stars, or glory?
I'll tell you, I'll tell you—thereof
Eat. Swallow. Absorb. Let bone
Be sustained thereof, let gristle
Toughen, flesh be more preciously
Gratified, muscle yearn in
Its strength. Let brain glow
In its own midnight of darkness,
Under its own inverted, bowl-shaped
Sky, skull-sky, let the heart
Rejoice.
            What other need now
Is possible to you but that
Of seeing life as glory?

Afterward

After the promise has been kept, or
Broken. After the sun

Has touched the peak westward and you suddenly
Realize that Time has cut another notch

In the stick with your name on it, and you wonder
How long before you will feel the need

For prayer. After you have stumbled on the obituary
Of a once-girl, photograph now unrecognizable,

Who, at night, used to come to your apartment and do everything but
It. Would fight like a tiger. Then weep.

Never married, but, as the paper says,
Made a brilliant career, also prominent in good works. After

You have, in shame, lain awake trying to account for
Certain deeds of vanity, weakness, folly, or

Neurosis, and have shuddered in disbelief. After
You have heard the unbearable, lonely wolf-howl of grief

In your heart, and walked a dark house, feet bare. After
You have looked down on the unimaginable expanse of polar

Icecap stretching in light of gray-green ambiguousness,
And, lulled by jet-hum, wondered if this

Is the only image of eternity. —Ah, menhirs, monoliths, and all
Such frozen thrusts of stone, arms in upward anguish of fantasy, images

*

By creatures hairy and humped, on heath, on hill, in holt
Raised! Oh, see

How a nameless skull, by weather uncovered or
The dateless winds,

In the moonlit desert, smiles, having been
So long alone. After all, are you ready

To return the smile? Try. Sit down by a great cactus,
While other cacti, near and as far as distance, lift up

Their arms, thorny and black, in ritual unresting above
Tangles of black shadow on white sand, to that great orb

Of ever out-brimming, unspooling light and glow, queenly for good
                                                    or evil, in
The forever sky. After you have sat

In company awhile, perhaps trust will grow.
Perhaps you can start a conversation of mutual comfort.

There must be so much to exchange.

Fear and Trembling

The sun now angles downward, and southward.
The summer, that is, approaches its final fulfillment.
The forest is silent, no wind-stir, bird-note, or word.
It is time to meditate on what the season has meant.

But what is the meaningful language for such meditation?
What is a word but wind through the tube of the throat?
Who defines the relation between the word *sun* and the sun?
What word has glittered on whitecap? Or lured blossom out?

Walk deeper, foot soundless, into the forest.
Stop, breath bated. Look southward, and up, where high leaves
Against sun, in vernal translucence, yet glow with the freshest
Young tint of the lost spring. Here now nothing grieves.

Can one, in fact, meditate in the heart, rapt and wordless?
Or find his own voice in the towering gust now from northward?
When boughs toss—is it in joy or pain and madness?
The gold leaf—is it whirled in anguish or ecstasy skyward?

Can the heart's meditation wake us from life's long sleep,
And instruct us how foolish and fond was our labor spent—
Us who now know that only at death of ambition does the deep
Energy crack crust, spurt forth, and leap

From grottoes, dark—and from the caverned enchainment?

From
BEING
HERE
Poetry 1977-1980

To Gabriel Thomas Penn (1836–1920)

There is in short no absolute Time Standard.

—*Van Nostrand's Scientific Encyclopedia*,
Fifth Edition, page 2203

I thirst to know the power and nature of time . . .

—St. Augustine: *Confessions*,
Book XI, Chapter 23
Translated by Albert C. Outler

Time is the dimension in which God strives to
define His own Being.

When Life Begins

Erect was the old Hellenistic head,
White-thatched in that dark cedar shade,
Curl-tangled the beard like skill-carved stone
With chisel-grooved shadow accenting the white.
The blue gaze fixed on a mythic distance.

That distance, a far hill's horizon, bulged
Past woods into the throbbing blue
Of a summer's afternoon. Our silence
Now seemed to have substantial life
That was the death of the pulse of Time.

One hand, gnarled, liver-blotched, but sinewed
From wrestling with the sleight of years,
Lay propped on a blue-jeaned knee and wrapped
Around a cob pipe, from which one thread
Of smoke, more blue than distance, rose
To twine into the cedar-dark.

The boy—he felt he wasn't there.
He felt that all reality
Had been cupboarded in that high head,
But now was absorbed into the abstractness
Of that blue gaze, so fixed and far,
Aimed lethally past the horizon's fact.

He thought all things that ever lived
Had gone to live behind that brow,
And in their infinite smallness slept
Until the old voice might wake them again
To strive in the past but passionate

*

Endeavor—hoofbeat at night, steel-clang,
Boom of the battery to take,
Far smoke seen long before you hear sound,

And before that, too, the gust of grape
Overhead, through oak leaves. Your stallion rears.

Your stallion rears—yes, it is *you*!

With your glasses you spot, from east, from west,
From woods-cover, skirmishers mincing out
On both flanks of that rise. Rifle-fire
Prickles the distance, noiseless, white.
Then a shell bursts over that fanged, far hill,
Single, annunciatory, like
A day-star over new Bethlehem.

In the country-quiet, momentarily
After that event renewed, one lone
Quail calls.

          And the old man, once he said
How a young boy, dying, broke into tears.
"Ain't scairt to die"—the boy's words—"it's jist
I ne'er had no chanst to know what tail's like."

Hunger and thirst, and the quavering yell
That more than bugle gave guts to a charge,
And once said: "My Mary, her hands were like silk,
But strong—and her mount on his shadow would dance."
Once said: "But things—they can seem like a dream."

Old eyelids shut the horizon out.
The boy sat and wondered when life would begin,
Nor knew that, beyond the horizon's heave,
Time crouched, like a great cat, motionless
But for tail's twitch. Night comes. Eyes glare.

Grackles, Goodbye

Black of grackles glints purple as, wheeling in sun-glare,
The flock splays away to pepper the blueness of distance.
Soon they are lost in the tracklessness of air.
I watch them go. I stand in my trance.

Another year gone. In trance of realization,
I remember once seeing a first fall leaf, flame-red, release
Bough-grip, and seek, through gold light of the season's sun,
Black gloss of a mountain pool, and there drift in peace.

Another year gone. And once my mother's hand
Held mine while I kicked the piled yellow leaves on the lawn
And laughed, not knowing some yellow-leaf season I'd stand
And see the hole filled. How they spread their obscene fake lawn.

Who needs the undertaker's sick lie
Flung thus in the teeth of Time, and earth's spin and tilt?
What kind of fool would promote that kind of lie?
Even sunrise and sunset convict the half-wit of guilt.

Grackles, goodbye! The sky will be vacant and lonely
Till again I hear your horde's rusty creak high above,
Confirming the year's turn and the fact that only, only,
In the name of Death do we learn the true name of Love.

Youthful Truth-Seeker, Half-Naked, at Night, Running Down Beach South of San Francisco

In dark, climbing up. Then down-riding the sand sluice
Beachward from dune-head. Running, feet bare on
Sand wet-packed and star-stung. Phlegm in lungs loose.
Though now tide turning, spume yet prickling air on

My chest, which naked, splits darkness. On the right hand,
Palisades of white-crashing breakers renew and stretch on
Into unmooned drama and distance.—To understand
Is impossible now. Flight from what? To what? And alone.

Far behind, the glow of the city of men fades slow.
And ahead, white surf and dark dunes in dimness are wed,
While Pacificward, fog, leagues afar, now threatens to grow,
But on I yet run, face up, stars shining above my wet head

Before they are swaddled in grayness, though grayness, perhaps,
Is what waits—after history, logic, philosophy too,
Even rhythm of lines that bring tears to the heart, and scraps
Of old wisdom that like broken bottles in darkness gleam at you.

What was the world I had lived in? Poetry, orgasm, joke:
And the joke the biggest on me, the laughing despair
Of a truth the heart might speak, but never spoke—
Like the twilit whisper of wings with no shadow on air.

You dream that somewhere, somehow, you may embrace
The world in its fullness and threat, and feel, like Jacob, at last
The merciless grasp of unwordable grace
Which has no truth to tell of future or past—

But only life's instancy, by daylight or night,
While constellations strive, or a warbler whets
His note, or the ice creaks blue in white-night Arctic light,
Or the maniac weeps—over what he always forgets.

*

So lungs aflame now, sand raw between toes,
And the city grows dim, dimmer still,
And the grind of breath and of sand is all one knows
Of what a man flees to, or from, in his angry need to fulfill

What?—On the beach flat I fall by the foam-frayed sea,
Which now and then brushes an outflung hand, as though
In tentative comfort, yet knowing itself to be
As ignorant as I, and as feckless also.

So I stare at the stars that remain, shut eyes, in dark press an ear
To sand, cold as cement, to apprehend,
Not merely the grinding of shingle and sea-slosh near,
But the groaning miles of depth where light finds its end.

Below all silken soil-slip, all crinkling earth-crust,
Far deeper than ocean, past rock that against rock grieves,
There at the globe's deepest dark and visceral lust,
Can I hear the *groan-swish* of magma that churns and heaves?

No word? No sign? Or is there a time and place—
Ice-peak or heat-simmered distance—where heart, like eye,
May open? But sleep at last—it has sealed up my face,
And last foam, retreating, creeps from my hand. It will dry,

While fog, star by star, imperially claims the night.
How long till dawn flushes dune-tops, or gilds beach-stones?
I stand up. Stand thinking, I'm one poor damn fool, all right.
Then ask, if years later, I'll drive again forth under stars, on tottering bones.

Why Have I Wandered the Asphalt of Midnight?

Why have I wandered the asphalt of midnight and not known why?
Not guilt, or joy, or expectation, or even to know how,
When clouds are tattered, the distance beyond screams its rage,
Or when fog breaks
To clarity—not even to know how the strict
Rearrangement of stars communicates
Their mystic message to
The attent corpuscles hurrying heartward, and from.

Why did I stand with no motion under
The spilt-ink darkness of spruces and try to hear,
In the soundlessness of falling snow,
The heartbeat I know as the only self
I know that I know, while History
Trails its meaning like old cobwebs
Caught in a cellar broom?

Why should I clamber the cliff now gone bone-white in moonlight?
Just to feel blood dry like a crust on hands, or watch
The moon lean westering to the next range,
The next, and beyond,
To wash the whole continent, like spume?
Why should I sit till from the next valley I hear
The great bear's autumnal sex-hoot
Or the glutted owl make utterance?

Why should I wander dark dunes till rollers
Boom in from China, stagger, and break
On the beach in frothed mania, while high to the right
The North Star holds steady enough to be Truth?

Yes, why, all the years, and places, and nights, have I
Wandered and not known the question I carried?

And carry? Yes, sometimes, at dawn,
I have seen the first farmer

Set bright the steel share to the earth, or met,
Snowshoed, the trapper just set on his dawn-rounds.
Or even, long back, on a streetcar
Bound cityward, watched some old workman
Lean over his lunch box, and yawn.

Sila

Sila, for the Eskimo, "is the air, not the sky; movement, not wind; the very breath of life, but not physical life; he is clear-sighted energy, activating intelligence; the powerful fluid circulating 'all around' and also within each individual . . ."
LAROUSSE WORLD MYTHOLOGY

Upgrade, past snow-tangled bramble, past
Deadfall snow-buried, there—
The ruin of old stonework, where man-heart
Long ago had once lifted
In joy, and back muscles strained. "Stay, Sila!" the boy
Commanded the tawny great husky, broad-chested,
That in harness yet stood, forward-leaning. The boy
Stamped his cross-countries. Stared
At the ruin. Thought:
*Two hundred years back—and it might
Have been me.*

And wondered what name the man
Might have had. Thought:
*Well, summer, I'll come
And hunt for the gravestones.* Then thought
How letters that crude must be weathered away—how deeper
A skull must be pulping to earth, and now grinless.
But thought: *At least, I can touch it, whatever
It is, stone or skull.*

Was young, then he thought, *young as me, maybe.*

Then felt muscles tighten and clinch
At a sudden impulse of surprise
To find here the old mark of life that for life
Once had sung, while the axe-edge glittered in sunlight.

Oh, what are the years! his heart cried, and he felt
His own muscles pulsing in joy, just as when
Hands clasp for the lift of the beauty of butt-swell.

Land is benched here, great beeches,
Gray, leafless, arising parklike and artful

From snow artificial as Christmas.
"Stay, Sila!" he called, and on level ground now
Slick-glided to where the blue gleam of ice-eyes
Looked up in his own, with a knowledge deeper than words.
He snapped harness loose, slipped out of cross-countries,
Wrapped cords at his waist, and—
The dog exploded.

From behind a beech deadfall, the doe, it had leaped,
Cow-awkward on earth, but magically airy in flight,
And weightless as wind, forelegs airward prowing
To seem as frail as a spider's, but hooves aglitter like glass
To cleave sunlight. Then,
Suddenly knifing the ice-crust as deep
As a trap, while the husky's wide paw-spread
Had opened like snowshoes behind.
Five leaps—and first blood, at a haunch,
Flesh laid back as though in a hunter's thin knife-slice.

Again, two more leaps, and white slash at belly—
Red line drawn clean on the curve. The boy's order
No use now: "Stay! Damn it, stay!" Until
Hand on harness, at last and too late, for
Red blood dripped now from white fang
To whiteness of snow, and eyes blue as steel drove into
The boy's eyes brain-deep, while, that instant,
All eons of friendship fled.
Then dog-eyes go earthward. The guts
Of the doe slip forth blue on the ice-crust.

The husky, stiff as in bronze cast, waits.

Only one thing to do. Who'd leave the doe there,
Dying slow into sunset, while all the small teeth—
Fox, field mouse, and wildcat—emerge
For their nocturnal feast? So the boy's knees bend,
Break the snow-crust like prayer,
And he cuddles the doe's head, and widening brown eyes
Seem ready, almost, to forgive.

*

He longs for connection, to give explanation. Sudden,
The head, now helpless, drops back on his shoulder. Twin eyes
Hold his own entrapped in their depth,
But his free hand, as though unaware,
Slides slow back
To grope for the knife-sheath.

The boy could not shut his eyes to the task,
As some fool girl might, but set
Eyes deeper in eyes, as he cradled the head, and gently
Held up the soft chin
To tauten the fullness of throat, and then,
As scrupulous as a well-trained tailor, set
The knife's needle point where acuteness
Would enter without prick of pain, and
Slashed in a single, deep motion.

He was sure that the doe
Never twitched.

On snow unconsciously heaped, he let down the head,
Aware even yet of the last embracement of gaze.
He watched, bewitched by the beauty, how blood flowed,
Red petal by petal, a great rose that bloomed where he stood.
How petal on petal, curve swelling past curve,
Gleamed forth at his feet on the snow,
And each petal sparkled with flicker of ice through the crimson,
As rays of last sun found a special glory in smallness.

He lifted his head, knife yet in hand, and westward
Fixed eyes beyond beech-bench to the snow-hatched
Stone thrust of the mountain, above which sky, too,
More majestically bloomed, but petals paler as higher—
The rose of the blood of the day. Still as stone,
So he stood. Then slowly—so slowly—
He raised the blade of the knife he loved honing, and wiped
The sweet warmness and wetness across his own mouth,
And set tongue to the edge of the silk-whetted steel.

*

He knew he knew something at last
That he'd never before known.
No name for it—no!

He snow-cleaned the knife. Sheathed it. Called: "Come!"
The dog, now docile, obeyed. With bare hands full of snow,
The boy washed him of blood and, comblike,
With fingers ennobled the ruff.

Then suddenly clasping the creature, he,
Over raw fur, past beeches, the mountain's snow-snag,
And the sky's slow paling of petals,
Cries out into vastness
Of silence: "Oh, world!"

He felt like a fool when tears came.

Some sixty years later, propped on death's pillow,
Again will he see that same scene, and try,
Heart straining, to utter that cry?—But
Cannot, breath short.

Vision

The vision will come—the Truth be revealed—but
Not even its vaguest nature you know—ah, truth

About what? But deep in the sibilant dark
That conviction irregularly

Gleams like fox-fire in sump-woods where,
In distance, lynx-scream or direful owl-stammer

Freezes the blood in a metaphysical shudder—which
Might be the first, feather-fine brush of Grace. Such

An event may come with night rain on roof, season changing
And bed too wide; or, say, when the past is de-fogged

And old foot tracks of folly show fleetingly clear before
Rationalization again descends, as from seaward.

Or when the shadow of pastness teasingly
Lifts and you recollect having caught—when, when?—

A glint of the nature of virtue like
The electrically exposed white of a flicker's

Rump feathers at the moment it flashes for the black thicket.
Or when, even, in a section of the city

Where no acquaintance would ever pass,
You watch snowflakes slash automobile lights

As you move toward the first
Illicit meeting, naturally at a crummy

*

Café. Your pace slows. You see her
Slip from the cab, dash for the door, dark fur coat

Collar up, head down. Inside,
As you order two highballs,

All eyes seem to focus on you. Drinks come, but
There is nothing to say. Hands

Do, damply, clasp—though no bed yet. Each stares
Into the other's eyes, desire like despair, and doom

Grows slow, and fat, and dark, like a burgundy begonia.
Soon you will watch the pale silken flash

Of well-turned ankles beneath dark fur,
As she hurries away on her stolen time, cab-hunting, and the future

Scarcely breathes. Your chest is a great clot. Perhaps then.
Oh, no. It may not happen, in fact, until

A black orderly, white-coated, on rubber soles, enters at 5 A.M.
The hospital room, suds and razor in hand, to shave,

With no word of greeting, the area the surgeon
Will penetrate. The robot departs. No one

Comes yet. Do not give up hope.
There is still time. Watch dawn blur the window.

Can it be that the vision has, long back, already come—
And you just didn't recognize it?

Cocktail Party

Beyond the haze of alcohol and syntax and
Flung gage of the girl's glance, and personal ambition,
You catch some eye-gleam, sense a faint
Stir, as of a beast in shadow. It may be Truth.

Into what distance all gabble crawls away!
You look, and thirty lips move without sound
As though something had gone wrong with the TV,
And you see, of a sudden, a woman's unheard laugh exposing

Glitter of gold in the mouth's dark ghetto like unspeakable
Obscenity, but not sound. You try
To speak, an urgency like hard phlegm
In your throat, but no sound comes. You quiver, thinking

Of the horror of Truth. It lies in wait—ha, ha!—
A pun—or rises, diaphanous, like
Smoke from the red-stained cigarette butt
Half-crushed in a carved gold ashtray.

In wait, it lies. Or like a tumor grows
Somewhere inside your brain. Oh, doctor, please, oh,
Remove it! Expense be damned, I only
See lips moving. I move my lips, but no

Sound comes, not even a lie. Yes, operate, then I
Can hear them—and tell them I love them. At least,
If we are all to be victims of Truth,
Let us be destroyed together in normal communication.

Or maybe I'm only a little drunk. Oh, waiter!

The Cross

Once, after storm, I stood at the cliff-head,
And up black basalt the sea's white claws
Still flung their eight fathoms up to have my blood.
In the blaze of new sun they leap in cruel whiteness,
Not forgiving me that their screaming lunges
Had nightlong been no more than a dream
In the tangle and warmth and breathless dark
Of love's huddle and sleep, while stars were black
And the tempest swooped down to snatch our tiles.

By three, wind down and sun still high,
I walked the beach of the little cove
Where scavengings of the waves were flung—
Old oranges, cordage, a bottle of beer
With the cap still tight, a baby-doll
But the face smashed in, a boom from some mast,
And most desperately hunched by volcanic stone
As though trying to cling in some final hope,
But drowned hours back you could be damned sure,
The monkey, wide-eyed, bewildered yet
By the terrible screechings and jerks and bangs,
And no friend to come and just say *ciao*.

I took him up, looked in his eyes,
As orbed as dark aggies, as bright as tears,
With a glaucous glint in deep sightlessness,
Yet still seeming human with all they had seen—
Like yours or mine, if luck had run out.

So, like a fool, I said *ciao* to him.

Under wet fur I felt how skin slid loose
On the poor little bones, and the delicate

Fingers yet grasped, at God knew what.
So I sat with him there, watching wind abate.

No funnel on the horizon showed.
And of course, no sail. And the cliff's shadow
Had found the cove. Well, time to go.

I took time, yes, to bury him,
In a scraped-out hole, little cairn on top.
And I enough fool to improvise
A cross—

Two sticks tied together to prop in the sand.

But what use that? The sea comes back.

Antinomy: Time and What Happened

1

Alone, alone, I lie. The canoe
On blackness floats. It must
Be so, for up to a certain point
All comes back clear. I saw,
At dock, the canoe, aluminum, rising ghost-white on blackness.
This much is true. Silent,
As entering air, the paddle, slow, dips. Silent,
I slide forth. Forth on,
Forth into,
What new dimension? Slow
As a dream, no ripple at keel, I move through
The stillness, on blackness, past hope or despair
Not relevant now to illusion I'd once
Thought I lived by. At last,
Shores absorbed in the blackness of forest, I lie down. High,
Stars stare down, and I
See them. I wonder
If they see me. If they do, do they know
What they see?

2

Do I hear stars speak in a whisper as gentle as breath
To the few reflections caught pale in the blackness beneath?
How still is the night! It must be their voices.
Then strangely a loon-cry glows ember-red,
And the ember in darkness dims
To a tangle of senses beyond windless fact or logical choices,
While out of Time, Timelessness brims
Like oil on black water, to coil out and spread
On the time that seems past and the time that may come,
And both the same under
The present's darkening dome.

131

3

A dog, in the silence, is barking a county away.
It is long yet till day.

4

As consciousness outward seeps, the dark seeps in.
As the self dissolves, realization surrenders its burden
And thus fulfills your fictionality.
Night wind is no more than unrippling drift.
The canoe, light as breath, moves in a dignity
As soundless as a star's mathematical shift
Reflected light-years away
In the lake's black parodic sky.

I wonder if this is I.

5

It is not long till day.

6

Dawn bursts like the birth pangs of your, and the world's, existence.
The future creeps into the blueness of distance.
Far back, scraps of memory hang, rag-rotten, on a rusting
                                        barbed-wire fence.

7

One crow, caw lost in the sky-peak's lucent trance,
Will gleam, sun-purpled, in its magnificence.

Safe in Shade

Eyes, not bleared but blue,
Of the old man, horizonward gazed—
As on horizons and years, long lost, but now
Projected from storage in that capacious skull.

He sat in his big chair propped
Against reddish tatter of
Bole-bark of the great cedar. I,
The boy who on the ground sat, waited.

I waited for him to speak.

I waited for him to come back to me
From the distances he traveled in.
I waited for him to speak. I saw
The cob pipe in the liver-spotted hand
Now propped on a knee, on the washed blue-jeans.
Smoke, frail, slow, blue—as blue
As the jeans but not the eyes—
Rose to thread the cedar-dark.
Around us in our shade and hush
Roared summer's fierce fecundity,
And the sun struck down,
In blare and dazzle, on the myth of the world, but we
Safe in the bourne of distance and shade,
Sat so silent that, from woods coming down
To the whitewashed fence but yards behind me,
I heard the secret murmur and hum
That in earth, on leaf, in air, seethed. Heard
One jay, outraged, scream.
The old blue eyes, they fixed on me.

I waited for him to speak. He spoke.

*

Now into the world hurled,
In later times and other places,
I lived but as man must
In all the garbled world's compulsions,
By fate perforce performed
Acts evil or good, or even
Both in the same act, in
That paradox the world exemplifies.

And Time, like wind-tattered smoke,
Blew by for one who, like all men, had flung,
In joy and man's maniacal
Rage, his blood
And the blind, egotistical, self-defining
Sperm into
That all-devouring, funnel-shaped, mad and high-spiraling,
Dark suction that
We have, as the Future, named.

Where is my cedar tree?

Where is the Truth—oh, unambiguous—
Thereof?

From
NOW AND
THEN
Poems 1976-1978

To Andrew Vincent Corry

. . . let the inhabitants of the rock sing . . .

—Isaiah 42:11

American Portrait: Old Style

I

Beyond the last house, where home was,
Past the marsh we found the old skull in, all nameless
And cracked in star-shape from a stone-smack,
Up the hill where the grass was tangled waist-high and wind-tousled,
To the single great oak that, in leaf-season, hung like
A thunderhead black against whatever blue the sky had,

And here, at the widest circumference of shade, when shade was,
Ran the trench, six feet long,
And wide enough for a man to lie down in,
In comfort, if comfort was still any object. No sign there
Of any ruined cabin or well, so Pap must have died of camp fever,
And the others pushed on, God knows where.

II

The Dark and Bloody Ground, so the teacher romantically said,
But one look out the window, and woods and ruined cornfields we saw:
A careless-flung corner of country, no hope and no history here.
No hope but the Pullman lights that swept
Night-fields—glass-glint from some farmhouse and flicker of ditches—
Or the night freight's moan on the rise where
You might catch a ride on the rods,
Just for hell, or if need had arisen.
No history either—no Harrod or Finley or Boone,
No tale how the Bluebellies broke at the Rebel yell and cold steel.

So we had to invent it all, our Bloody Ground, K and I,
And him the best shot in ten counties and could call any bird-note back,
But school out, not big enough for the ballgame,
And in the full tide of summer, not ready
For the twelve-gauge yet, or even a job, so what

137

Can you do but pick up your BBs and Benjamin,
Stick corn pone in pocket, and head out
"To Rally in the Cane-Brake and Shoot the Buffalo"—
As my grandfather's cracked old voice would sing it
From days of his own grandfather—and often enough
It was only a Plymouth Rock or maybe a fat Dominecker
That fell to the crack of the unerring Decherd.

III

Yes, imagination is strong. But not strong enough in the face of
The sticky feathers and BBs a mother's hand held out.
But no liberal concern was evinced for a Redskin,
As we trailed and out-tricked the sly Shawnees
In a thicket of ironweed, and I wrestled one naked
And slick with his bear grease, till my hunting knife
Bit home, and the tomahawk
Slipped from his hand. And what mother cared about Bluebellies
Who came charging our trench? But we held
To pour the last volley at face-gape before
The tangle and clangor of bayonet.

Yes, a day is merely forever
In memory's shiningness,
And a year but a gust or a gasp
In the summer's heat of Time, and in that last summer
I was almost ready to learn
What imagination is—it is only
The lie we must learn to live by, if ever
We mean to live at all. Times change.
Things change. And K up and gone, and the summer
Gone, and I longed to know the world's name.

IV

Well, what I remember most
In a world long Time-pale and powdered
Like a vision still clinging to plaster
Set by Piero della Francesca
Is how K, through lane-dust or meadow,

Seemed never to walk, but float
With a singular joy and silence,
In his cloud of bird dogs, like angels,
With their eyes on his eyes like God,
And the sun on his uncut hair bright
As he passed through the ramshackle town and odd folks there
With coats on and vests and always soft gabble of money—
Polite in his smiling, but never much to say.

V

To pass through to what? No, not
To some wild white peak dreamed westward,
And each sunrise a promise to keep. No, only
The Big Leagues, not even a bird dog,
And girls that popped gum while they screwed.

Yes, this was his path, and no batter
Could do what booze finally did:
Just blow him off the mound—but anyway,
He had always called it a fool game, just something
For children who hadn't yet dreamed what
A man is, or barked a squirrel, or raised
A single dog from a pup.

VI

And I, too, went on my way, the winning and losing, or what
Is sometimes of all things the worst, the not knowing
One thing from the other, nor knowing
How the teeth in Time's jaw all snag backward
And whatever enters therein
Has less hope of remission than shark-meat,

And on Sunday afternoon, in the idleness of summer,
I found his farm, and him home there,
With the bird dogs crouched round in the grass
And their eyes on his eyes as he whispered
Whatever to bird dogs it was.
Then yelled: "Well, for Christ's sake—it's you!"

*

Yes, me, for Christ's sake, and some sixty
Years blown like a hurricane past! But what can you say—
Can you say—when *all-to-be-said* is the *done?*
So our talk ran to buffalo-hunting, and the look on his mother's face
When she held the BBs out.

And the sun sank slow as he stood there,
All Indian-brown from waist up, who never liked tops to his pants,
And standing nigh straight, but the arms and the pitcher's
Great shoulders, they were thinning to old-man thin.
Sun low, all silence, then sudden:
"But, Jesus," he cried, "what makes a man do what he does—
Him living until he dies!"

Sure, all of us live till we die, but bingo!
Like young David at brookside, he swooped down,
Snatched a stone, wound up, and let fly,
And high on a pole over yonder the big brown insulator
Simply exploded. "See—I still got control!" he said.

    VII

Late, late, toward sunset, I wandered
Where old dreams had once been Life's truth, and where
I saw the trench of our valor, now nothing
But a ditch full of late-season weed-growth,
Beyond the rim of shade.

There was nobody there, hence no shame to be saved from, so I
Just lie in the trench on my back and see high,
Beyond the tall ironweed stalks, or oak leaves
If I happened to look that way,
How the late summer's thinned-out sky moves,
Drifting on, drifting on, like forever,
From *where* on to *where,* and I wonder
What it would be like to die,
Like the nameless old skull in the swamp, lost,
And know yourself dead lying under
The infinite motion of sky.

VIII

But why should I lie here longer?
I am not dead yet, though in years,
And the world's way is yet long to go,
And I love the world even in my anger,
And that's a hard thing to outgrow.

Amazing Grace in the Back Country

In the season of late August star-fall,
When the first crickets crinkled the dark,
There by woods, where oaks of the old forest-time
Yet swaggered and hulked over upstarts, the tent
Had been pitched, no bigger than one of
Some half-bankrupt carnival come
To town with fat lady, human skeleton, geek,
Man-woman and moth-eaten lion, and one
Boa constrictor for two bits seen
Fed a young calf or what; plus a brace
Of whores to whom menopause now
Was barely a memory, one with gold teeth and one
With game gam, but both
With aperture ready to serve
Any late-lingerers, and leave
A new and guaranteed brand of syphilis handy—yes,

The tent old and yellowed and patched,
Lit inside by three wire-hung gasoline lamps
That outside, through threadbare canvas, were muted to gold.
Here no carnival now—the tabernacle
To the glory of God the Most High, for now corn
Was laid by, business slack, such business as was, and
The late-season pain gnawing deep at the human bone
As the season burned on to its end.

God's Word and His glory—and I, aged twelve,
Sat there while an ex-railroad engineer
Turned revivalist shouted the Threat and the Promise, with sweat
On his brow, shirt plastered to belly, and
Eyes a-glaze with the mania of joy.

And now by my knees crouched some old-fool dame
In worn-out black silk, there crouching with tears

In her eyes as she tugged me to kneel
And save my pore twelve-year-old soul
Before too late. She wept.
She wept and she prayed, and I knew I was damned,
Who was guilty of all short of murder,
At least in my heart and no alibi there, and once
I had walked down a dark street, lights out in houses,
Uttering, "Lust—lust—lust,"
Like an invocation, out loud—and the word
So lovely, fresh-minted.

I saw others fall as though stricken. I heard
The shout of salvation. I stared
In the red-rimmed, wet eyes of the crazy old dame,
Whose name I never remembered, but knew
That she loved me—the Pore Little Lamb—and I thought
How old bones now creaked in God's name.

But the Pore Little Lamb, he hardened his heart,
Like a flint nigger-head rounded slick in a creek-bed
By generations of flood, and suddenly
I found myself standing, then
Ran down an aisle, and outside,
Where cool air and dark filled my lungs, and fifty
Yards off, with my brow pressed hard
On the scaly bark of a hickory tree,
Vomited. Fumbling
In darkness, I found the spring
And washed my mouth. Humped there,

And knowing damnation, I stared
Through interstices of black brush to the muted gold glow
Of God's canvas, till in
The last hymn of triumph rose voices, and hearts
Burst with joy at amazing grace so freely given,
And moving on into darkness,

Voices sang of amazing grace, singing as they
Straggled back to the village, where voice after voice died away,
As singer by singer, in some dark house,
Found bed and lay down,

And tomorrow would rise and do all the old things to do,
Until that morning they would not rise, not ever.

And now, when all voices were stilled and the lamps
Long out in the tent, and stars
Had changed place in the sky, I yet lay
By the spring with one hand in cold black water
That showed one star in reflection, alone—and lay
Wondering and wondering how many
A morning would I rise up to greet,
And what grace find.

But that was long years ago. I was twelve years old then.

Boy Wandering in Simms' Valley

Through brush and love-vine, well blooded by blackberry thorn
Long dry past prime, under summer's late molten light
And past the last rock-slide at ridge-top and stubborn,
Raw tangle of cedar, I clambered, breath short and spit white

From lung-depth. Then down the lone valley, called Simms' Valley still,
Where Simms, long back, had nursed a sick wife till she died.
Then turned out his spindly stock to forage at will,
And took down his twelve-gauge, and simply lay down by her side.

No kin they had, and nobody came just to jaw.
It was two years before some straggling hunter sat down
On the porch-edge to rest, then started to prowl. He saw
What he saw, saw no reason to linger, so high-tailed to town.

A dirt-farmer needs a good wife to keep a place trim,
So the place must have gone to wrack with his old lady sick.
And when I came there, years later, old furrows were dim,
And dimmer in fields where grew maples and such, a span thick.

So for years the farm had contracted: now barn down, and all
The yard back to wilderness gone, and only
The house to mark human hope, but ready to fall.
No buyer at tax-sale, it waited, forgotten and lonely.

I stood in the the bedroom upstairs, in lowering sun,
And saw sheets hang spiderweb-rotten, and blankets a mass
Of what weather and leaves from the broken window had done,
Not to mention the rats. And thought what had there come to pass.

But lower was sinking the sun. I shook myself,
Flung a last glance around, then suddenly
Saw the old enameled bedpan, high on a shelf.
I stood still again, as the last sun fell on me,

And stood wondering what life is, and love, and what they may be.

Red-Tail Hawk and Pyre of Youth

To Harold Bloom

1

Breath clamber-short, face sun-peeled, stones
Loose like untruth underfoot, I
Had just made the ridge crest, and there,
Opening like joy, the unapprehensible purity
Of afternoon flooded, in silver,
The sky. It was
The hour of stainless silver just before
The gold begins.

Eyes, strangely heavy like lead,
Drew down to the .30-30 hung on my hand
As on a crooked stick, in growing wonder
At what it might really be. It was as though
I did not know its name. Nor mine. Nor yet had known
That all is only
All, and part of all. No wind
Moved the silver light. No movement,

Except for the center of
That convex perfection, not yet
A dot even, nameless, no color, merely
A shadowy vortex of silver. Then,
In widening circles—oh, nearer!
And suddenly I knew the name, and saw,
As though seeing, it come toward me,
Unforgiving, the hot blood of the air:
Gold eyes, unforgiving, for they, like God, see all.

2

There was no decision in the act,
There was no choice in the act—the act impossible but
Possible. I screamed, not knowing

From what emotion, as at that insane range
I pressed the cool, snubbed
Trigger. Saw
The circle
Break.

3

Heart leaping in joy past definition, in
Eyes tears past definition, by rocky hill and valley
Already dark-devoured, the bloody
Body already to my bare flesh embraced, cuddled
Like babe to heart, and my heart beating like love:
Thus homeward.

But nobody there.

So at last
I dared stare in the face—the lower beak drooping,
As though from thirst, eyes filmed.
Like a secret, I wrapped it in newspaper quickly
And hid it deep
In the ice chest.

Too late to start now.

4

Up early next morning, with
My father's old razor laid out, the scissors,
Pliers and needles, waxed thread,
The burlap and salt, the arsenic and clay,
Steel rods, thin, and glass eyes
Gleaming yellow. Oh, yes,
I knew my business. And at last a red-tail—

Oh, king of the air!

And at that miraculous range.

How my heart sang!

*

Till all was ready—skull now well scraped
And with arsenic dried, and all flesh joints, and the cape
Like a carapace feathered in bronze, and naturally anchored
At beak and at bone joints, and steel
Driven through to sustain wing and bone
And the clay-burlap body there within.
It was molded as though for that moment to take to the air—though,
In God's truth, the chunk of poor wingless red meat,
The model from which all was molded, lay now
Forever earthbound, fit only
For dog tooth, not sky.

5

Year after year, in my room, on the tallest of bookshelves,
Regal, it perched on its bough-crotch to guard
Blake and *Lycidas*, Augustine, Hardy and *Hamlet*,
Baudelaire and Rimbaud, and I knew that the yellow eyes,
Unsleeping, stared as I slept.

Till I slept in that room no more.

6

Years pass like a dream, are a dream, and time came
When my mother was dead, father bankrupt, and whiskey
Hot in my throat while there for the last

Time I lay, and my heart
Throbbed slow in the
Meaningless motion of life, and with
Eyes closed I knew
That yellow eyes somewhere, unblinking, in vengeance stared.

Or *was* it vengeance? What could I know?

Could Nature forgive, like God?

7

That night in the lumber room, late,
I found him—the hawk, feathers shabby, one
Wing bandy-banged, one foot gone sadly
Askew, one eye long gone—and I reckoned
I knew how it felt with one gone.

And all relevant items I found there: my first book of Milton,
The *Hamlet*, the yellow, leaf-dropping Rimbaud, and a book
Of poems friends and I had printed in college, not to mention
The collection of sexual Japanese prints—strange sex
Of mechanical sexlessness. And so made a pyre for
The hawk that, though gasoline-doused and wing-dragging,
Awaited, with what looked like pride,
The match.

8

Flame flared. Feathers first, and I flinched, then stood
As the steel wire warped red to defend
The shape designed godly for air. But
It fell with the mass, and I
Did not wait.

What left
To do but walk in the dark, and no stars?

9

Some dreams come true, some no.
But I've waked in the night to see
High in the late and uncurdled silver of summer
The pale vortex appear once again—and you come
And always the rifle swings up, though with
The weightlessness now of dream,
The old .30-30 that knows
How to bind us in air-blood and earth-blood together
In our commensurate fate,
Whose name is a name beyond joy.

149

And I pray that in some last dream or delusion,
While hospital wheels creak beneath
And the nurse's soles make their *squeak-squeak* like mice,
I'll again see the first small silvery swirl
Spin outward and downward from sky-height
To bring me the truth in blood-marriage of earth and air—
And all will be as it was
In that paradox of unjoyful joyousness,
Till the dazzling moment when I, a last time, must flinch
From the regally feathered gasoline flare
Of youth's poor, angry, slapdash, and ignorant pyre.

Star-Fall

In that far land, and time, near the castrated drawbridge where
For four bloody centuries garbage
In the moat's depth had been spilled
To stink, but most at the broiling noontide—
There we, now at midnight, lay.

We lay on the dry grass of August, high
On our cliff, and the odor we caught was of bruised
Rosemary at pathside, not garbage, and sometimes
The salt air of sea, and the only sound to our ears
Was the slap and hiss far below, for the sea has never forgiven
The nature of stone.

We did not lie close, and for hours
The only contact was fingers, and motionless they.
For what communication
Is needed if each alone
Is sunk and absorbed into
The mass and matrix of Being that defines
Nature of all?

We lay in the moonless night,
Felt earth beneath us swing,
Watched the falling stars of the season. They fell
Like sparks in a shadowy, huge smithy, with
The clang of the hammer unheard.

Far off in the sea's matching midnight,
Lights of fishing boats marked their unfabled constellations.

We found nothing to say, for what can a voice say when
The world is a voice, no ear needing?

We lay watching stars as they fell.

151

Youth Stares at Minoan Sunset

On the lap of the mountain meadow,
At the break of the Cretan cliff-quarry where
Venetians had once sawed their stone, soft
Nag of surf far below foot, he
Stares seaward the distance to sunset.

The sky is rose-hearted, immense, undisturbed.
In that light the youth's form is black, without motion,
And birds, gull nor other, have no transaction
In the inflamed emptiness of sky. Mountainward,
No bird cries. We had called once,
But we were too far, too far.

Molten and massy, of its own weight flattened,
The sun accelerates downward, the sea,
From general slate-blue, flaming upward.
Contact is made at the horizon line.

On that line, one instant, one only,
The great coin, flame-massy and with
The frail human figure thereon minted black,
Balances. Suddenly is gone. A gull
Defiles at last the emptiness of air.

We are closer now. The black
Silhouette, yet small, stares seaward. To our cry
It does not turn. Later,
It will, and turning, see us with a slow
And pitying happiness of recognition born of
A knowledge we do not yet have. Or have forgotten.

He spreads his arms to the sky as though he loves it—and us.

He is so young.

Ah, Anima!

Watch the great bough lashed by wind and rain. Is it
A metaphor for your soul—or Man's—or even

Mine in the hurricane of Time? Now,
In the gray and splintered light, in the scything

Tail of the hurricane, miles of forest around us
Heave like the sea, and the gray underside of leaf is exposed

Of every tree, non-coniferous. The tall
Pines blackly stagger. Beyond,

The bulk and backdrop of mountain is
Obscured. Can you locate yourself

On the great chart of history?
In the distance a tree crashes.

Empires have fallen, and the stream
Gnashes its teeth with the *klang* of boulders.

Later, sleep. Tomorrow, help
Will come. The Governor promises. Roads will be rebuilt,

And houses. Food distributed. But, meanwhile, sleep
Is a disaster area, too. You have lain down

In the shards of Time and the un-roar of the wind of being,
And when, in the dark, you wake, with only

The *klang* of distant boulders in your ears,
You may wish that you, even in the wrack and dark pelt of storm,

*

Had run forth, screaming as wind snatched your breath away
Until you were nameless—oh, anima!—and only

Your mouth, rounded, is in the night there, the utterance gone. Perhaps
That is the only purity—to leave

The husk behind, and leap
Into the blind and antiseptic anger of air.

Unless

All will be in vain unless—unless what? Unless
You realize that what you think is Truth is only

A husk for something else. Which might,
Shall we say, be called energy, as good a word as any. As when

The rattlesnake, among desert rocks
And Freudian cactus tall in moonlight,

Scrapes off the old integument, and flows away,
Clean and lethal and gleaming like water over moon-bright sand,

Unhusked for its mission. Oh, *neo nato!* fanged, unforgiving,
We worship you for what you are. In the morning,

In the ferocity of daylight, the old skin
Will be translucent and abstract, like Truth. The mountains,

In distance, will glitter like diamonds, or salt.
They too will, in that light, seem abstract.

At night I have stood there, and the wide world
Was flat and circular under the storm of the

Geometry of stars. The mountains, in starlight, were black
And black-toothed to define the enormous circle

Of desert of which I was the center. This
Is one way to approach the question.

All is in vain unless you can, motionless, standing there,
Breathe with the rhythm of stars.

*

You cannot, of course, see your own face, but you know that it,
Lifted, is stripped to white bone by starlight. This is happening.

This is happiness.

The Mission

In the dark kitchen the electric icebox rustles.
It whispers like the interior dialogue of guilt and extenuation,
And I wake from a dream of horses. They do not know
I am dreaming of them. By this time they must be long dead.

Behind barbed wire, in fog off the sea, they stand.
Two clumps of horses, uncavorting, like gray stone, stand,
Heavy manes unrustling in even the gray sea wind.
The sea is gray. Night falls. Later, the manes will rustle,

But ever so little, in new wind lifting off the Bay of Biscay. But no—
They are dead. *La boucherie chevaline*, in the village,
Has a gold horse-head above the door. I wake
From my dream, and know that the shadow

Of the great spruce close by my house must be falling
Black on the white roof of winter. The spruce
Wants to hide the house from the moon, for
The moon's intentions have never been quite clear.

The spruce does not know that a secret square of moonlight lies
                                                        cunningly on
The floor by my bed, and I watch it and think how,
On the snow-locked mountain, deep in a fissure
Under the granite ledge, the bear

Huddles inside his fur like an invalid inside
A charity-ward blanket. Fat has thinned on bone, and the fur
Is too big for him now. He stirs in sleep, farts
Gently in the glacial blackness of the cave. The eyes

Do not open. Outside, in moonlight,
The ledges are bearded with ice, and the brook,
Black, crawls under ice. It has a mission, but,
In that blackness, has forgotten what. I, too,

*

157

Have forgotten the nature of my own mission. This
May be fortunate, for if I stare at the dark ceiling
And try to remember, I do not have to go back to sleep,
And not sleeping, will not again dream

Of clumps of horses, fog-colored in sea fog, rumps
To the sea wind, standing like stone primitively hewn,
While the fields, gray, stretch beyond them, and distance dies.
Perhaps that lost mission is to try to understand

The possibility of joy in the world's tangled and hieroglyphic beauty.

How to Tell a Love Story

There is a story that I must tell, but
The feeling in my chest is too tight, and innocence
Crawls through the tangles of fear, leaving,
Dry and translucent, only its old skin behind like
A garter snake's annual discard in the ground juniper. If only

I could say just the first word with breath
As sweet as a babe's and with no history—but, Christ,
If there is no history there is no story.
And no Time, no word.
For then there is nothing for a word to be about, a word

Being frozen Time only, and I have dived deep
Where light faded from gold to dark blue, and darker below,
And my chest was filled with a story like innocence,
But I rose, rose up, and plunged into light-blaze brutal as blackness,
And the sky whirled like fireworks. Perhaps I could then have begun it.

If only the first word would come and untwist my tongue!
Then the story might grow like Truth, or a tree, and your face
Would lean at me. If only the story could begin when all truly began,
White surf and a storm of sunlight, you running ahead and a smile
Back-flung—but then, how go on? For what would it mean?

Perhaps I can't say the first word till I know what it all means.
Perhaps I can't know till the doctor comes in and leans.

Little Black Heart of the Telephone

That telephone keeps screaming its little black heart out:
Nobody there? Oh, nobody's there!—and the blank room bleeds
For the poor little black bleeding heart of the telephone.
I, too, have suffered. I know how it feels
When you scream and scream, and nobody's there.
I am feeling that way this goddam minute,
If for no particular reason.

Tell the goddam thing to shut up! Only
It's not ringing now at all, but I
Can scrutinize it and tell that it's thinking about
Ringing, and just any minute, I know.
So, you demand, *the room's not empty, you're there?*
Yes, I'm here, but it might start screaming just after
I've gone out the door, in my private silence.

Or if I stayed here I mightn't answer, might pretend
Not to be here at all, or just be part of the blankness
The room is, as the blankness
Bleeds for the little bleeding black heart
Of the telephone. If, in fact, it should scream,
My heart would bleed too, for I know how pain can't find words.
Or sometimes is afraid to find them.

I tell you because I know you will understand.
I know you have screamed: *Nobody there? Oh, nobody's there!*
You've looked up at stars lost in blankness that bleeds
Its metaphysical blood, but not of redemption.
Have you ever stopped by the roadside at night, and couldn't
Remember your name, and breath
Came short? Or at night waked up with a telephone screaming,
And covered your head, afraid to answer?

*

160

Anyway, in broad daylight, I'm now in the street,
And no telephone anywhere near, or even
Thinking about me. But tonight, back in bed, I may dream
Of a telephone screaming its little black heart out,
In an empty room, toward sunset,
While a year-old newspaper, yellowing, lies on the floor, and velvety
Dust thick over everything, especially
On the black telephone, on which no thumb-print has,
For a long time now, been visible.

In my dream I wonder why, long since, it's not been disconnected.

Heart of Autumn

Wind finds the northwest gap, fall comes.
Today, under gray cloud-scud and over gray
Wind-flicker of forest, in perfect formation, wild geese
Head for a land of warm water, the *boom*, the lead pellet.

Some crumple in air, fall. Some stagger, recover control,
Then take the last glide for a far glint of water. None
Knows what has happened. Now, today, watching
How tirelessly *V* upon *V* arrows the season's logic,

Do I know my own story? At least, they know
When the hour comes for the great wing-beat. Sky-strider,
Star-strider—they rise, and the imperial utterance,
Which cries out for distance, quivers in the wheeling sky.

That much they know, and in their nature know
The path of pathlessness, with all the joy
Of destiny fulfilling its own name.
I have known time and distance, but not why I am here.

Path of logic, path of folly, all
The same—and I stand, my face lifted now skyward,
Hearing the high beat, my arms outstretched in the tingling
Process of transformation, and soon tough legs,

With folded feet, trail in the sounding vacuum of passage,
And my heart is impacted with a fierce impulse
To unwordable utterance—
Toward sunset, at a great height.

From
CAN I SEE
ARCTURUS FROM
WHERE I STAND?

Poems 1975

Is *was* but a word for wisdom, its price?

—"Rattlesnake Country"

A Way to Love God

Here is the shadow of truth, for only the shadow is true.
And the line where the incoming swell from the sunset Pacific
First leans and staggers to break will tell all you need to know
About submarine geography, and your father's death rattle
Provides all biographical data required for the *Who's Who* of the dead.

I cannot recall what I started to tell you, but at least
I can say how night-long I have lain under stars and
Heard mountains moan in their sleep. By daylight,
They remember nothing, and go about their lawful occasions
Of not going anywhere except in slow disintegration. At night
They remember, however, that there is something they cannot remember,
So moan. Theirs is the perfected pain of conscience, that
Of forgetting the crime, and I hope you have not suffered it. I have.

I do not recall what had burdened my tongue, but urge you
To think on the slug's white belly, how sick-slick and soft,
On the hairiness of stars, silver, silver, while the silence
Blows like wind by, and on the sea's virgin bosom unveiled
To give suck to the wavering serpent of the moon; and,
In the distance, in *plaza, piazza, place, platz,* and square,
Boot heels, like history being born, on cobbles bang.

Everything seems an echo of something else.

And when, by the hair, the headsman held up the head
Of Mary of Scots, the lips kept on moving,
But without sound. The lips,
They were trying to say something very important.

But I had forgotten to mention an upland
Of wind-tortured stone white in darkness, and tall, but when
No wind, mist gathers, and once on the Sarré at midnight,
I watched the sheep huddling. Their eyes

Stared into nothingness. In that mist-diffused light their eyes
Were stupid and round like the eyes of fat fish in muddy water,
Or of a scholar who has lost faith in his calling.

Their jaws did not move. Shreds
Of dry grass, gray in gray mist-light, hung
From the side of a jaw, unmoving.

You would think that nothing would ever again happen.

That may be a way to love God.

Evening Hawk

From plane of light to plane, wings dipping through
Geometries and orchids that the sunset builds,
Out of the peak's black angularity of shadow, riding
The last tumultuous avalanche of
Light above pines and the guttural gorge,
The hawk comes.

              His wing
Scythes down another day, his motion
Is that of the honed steel-edge, we hear
The crashless fall of stalks of Time.

The head of each stalk is heavy with the gold of our error.

Look! Look! he is climbing the last light
Who knows neither Time nor error, and under
Whose eye, unforgiving, the world, unforgiven, swings
Into shadow.

              Long now,
The last thrush is still, the last bat
Now cruises in his sharp hieroglyphics. His wisdom
Is ancient, too, and immense. The star
Is steady, like Plato, over the mountain.

If there were no wind we might, we think, hear
The earth grind on its axis, or history
Drip in darkness like a leaking pipe in the cellar.

Paradox

Running ahead beside the sea,
You turned and flung a smile, like spray.
It glittered like tossed spray in the sunlight.
Yes, well I remember, to this day,
That glittering ambiguity.

I saw, when your foot fulfilled its stride,
How the sand, compressed, burst to silver light,
But when I had reached that aureoled spot
There was only another in further flight:
And bright hair, wind-strung, to tease the sun's pride.

Yes, far away and long ago,
In another land, on another shore,
That race you won—even as it was lost,
For if I caught you, one moment more,
You had fled my grasp, up and to go

With glowing pace and the smile that mocks
Pursuit down whatever shore reflects
Our flickering passage through the years,
As we enact our more complex
Version of Zeno's paradox.

Midnight Outcry

Torn from the dream-life, torn from the life-dream,
Beside him in darkness, the cry bursts: *Oh*!
Endearment and protest—they avail
Nothing against whatever is so
Much deeper and darker than anything love may redeem.

He lies in the dark and tries to remember
How godlike to strive in passion and sweat,
But fears to awaken and clasp her, lest
Their whole life be lost, for he cannot forget
That the depths that cry rose from might shrivel a heart, or member.

How bright dawns morning!—how sweetly the face
Inclines over the infant to whom she gives suck.
So his heart leaps in joy, but remembering
That echo of fate beyond faith or luck,
He fixes his studious gaze on the scene to trace

In the least drop spilled between nipple and the ferocious
Little lip-suction, some logic, some white
Spore of the human condition that carries,
In whiteness, the dark need that only at night
Finds voice—one only and always strange to us.

The day wore on, and he would ponder,
Lifting eyes from his work, thinking, thinking,
Of the terrible distance in love, and the pain,
Smiling back at the sunlit smile, even while shrinking
From recall of the nocturnal timbre, and the dark wonder.

Old Nigger on One-Mule Cart Encountered Late at Night When Driving Home from Party in the Back Country

Flesh, of a sudden, gone nameless in music, flesh
Of the dancer, under your hand, flowing to music, girl-
Flesh sliding, flesh flowing, sweeter than
Honey, slicker than Essolube, over
The music-swayed, delicate trellis of bone
That is white in secret flesh-darkness. What
The music, it says: *no name, no name!*—only
That movement under your hand, what
It is, and no name, and you shut your eyes, but
The music, it stops. O.K. Silence
Rages, it ranges the world, it will
Devour us, for
That sound I do now hear is not external, is
Simply the crinkle and crepitation,
Like crickets gone nuts, of
Booze in the blood. *Goodnight! Goodnight!*

I can't now even remember the name of the dancer, but

I must try to tell you what, in July, in Louisiana,
Night is. No moon, but stars whitely outrageous in
Blackness of velvet, the long lane ahead
Whiter than snow, wheels soundless in deep dust, dust
Pluming whitely behind, and ahead all
The laneside hedges and weed-growth
Long since powdered whiter than star-dust, or frost, but air
Hot. The night pants hot like a dog, it breathes
Off the blossoming bayou like the expensive whiff
Of floral tributes at a gangster's funeral in N.O.,
It breathes the smell love makes in darkness, and far off,
In the great swamp, an owl cries,
And does not stop. At the sharp right turn,
Hedge-blind, which you take too fast,
There it is: death-trap.

*

Oh the fool-nigger—ass-hole wrong side of
The road, naturally: And the mule-head
Thrusts at us, and ablaze in our headlights,
Outstaring from primal bone-blankness and the arrogant
Stupidity of skull snatched there
From darkness and the saurian stew of pre-history.
For an instant—the eyes. The eyes,
They blaze from the incandescent magma
Of mule-brain. Thus mule-eyes. Then
Man-eyes, not blazing, white-bulging
In black face, in black night, and man-mouth
Wide open, the shape of an *O*, for the scream
That does not come. Even now,
That much in my imagination, I see. But also
The cargo of junk the black face blooms amidst—
Rusted bed-springs on end, auto axle at God-knows-what
Angle up-canted, barbed wire on a fence rail wound,
Lengths of stove pipe beat-up. God-yes,
A death-trap. But
I snatch the wheel left in a dust-skid,
Smack into the ditch, but the ditch
Shallow, and so, not missing a beat, I'm out
And go on, and he's left alone on his cart there
Unmoving, and dust of the car's passage settles
White on sweat-sticky skin, black, of the forehead, and on
The already gray head. This,
Of course, under the high stars.

Perhaps he had screamed, after all.

And go on: to the one last drink, sweat-grapple in darkness, then
Sleep. But only until
The hour when small, though disturbing, gastric shifts
Are experienced, the hour when the downy
Throat of the swamp owl vibrates to the last
Predawn cry, the hour
When joy-sweat, or night-sweat, has dried to a microscopic
Crust on the skin, and some
Recollection of childhood brings tears
To dark-wide eyes, and the super-ego

Again throws the switch for the old recorded harangue.
Until waking, that is—and I wake to see
Floating in darkness above the bed the
Black face, eyes white-bulging, mouth shaped like an *O*, and so
Get up, get paper and pencil, and whittle away at
The poem. Give up. Back to bed. And remember
Now only the couplet of what
Had aimed to be—Jesus Christ—a sonnet:
One of those who gather junk and wire to use
For purposes that we cannot peruse.

As I said, Jesus Christ. But

Moved on through the years. Am here. Another
Land, another love, and in such latitude, having risen
In darkness, feet bare to cold boards, stare,
Through ice-glitter of glass and air purer
Than absolute zero, into
The white night and star-crackling sky over
The snow-mountain. Have you ever,
At night, stared into the snow-filled forest and felt
The impulse to flee there? Enter there? Be
There and plunge naked
Through snow, through drifts floundering, white
Into whiteness, among
Spectral great beech-boles, birch-whiteness, black jag
Of shadow, black spruce-bulks snow-shouldered, floundering
Upward and toward the glacial assertion that
The mountain is? Have you ever
Had the impulse to stretch forth your hand over
The bulge of forest and seize trees like the hair
Of a head you would master? Well,
We are entitled to our fantasies, for life
Is only the fantasy that has happened to us, and

In God's name. But

In the lyrical logic and nightmare astuteness that
Is God's name, by what magnet, I demand,
Are the iron and out-flung filings of our lives, on
A sheet of paper, blind-blank as Time, snapped

Into a polarized pattern—and I see,
By a bare field that yearns pale in starlight, the askew
Shack. He arrives there. Unhitches the mule.
Stakes it out. Between cart and shack,
Pauses to make water, and while
The soft, plopping sound in deep dust continues, his face
Is lifted into starlight, calm as prayer. He enters
The dark shack, and I see
A match spurt, then burn down, die.

The last glow is reflected on the petal-pink
And dark horn-crust of the thumbnail.

And so I say:
Brother, Rebuker, my Philosopher past all
Casuistry, will you be with me when
I arrive and leave my own cart of junk
Unfended from the storm of starlight and
The howl, like wind, of the world's monstrous blessedness,
To enter, by a bare field, a shack unlit?
Entering into that darkness to fumble
My way to a place to lie down, but holding,
I trust, in my hand, a name—
Like a shell, a dry flower, a worn stone, a toy—merely
A hard-won something that may, while Time
Backward unblooms out of time toward peace, utter
Its small, sober, and inestimable
Glow, trophy of truth.

Can I see Arcturus from where I stand?

From
OR ELSE–
Poem/Poems 1968-1974

To Cesare and Rysia Lombroso

He clave the rocks in the wilderness, and gave
them drink as out of the great depths.

—Psalms 78:15

The Nature of a Mirror

The sky has murder in the eye, and I
Have murder in the heart, for I
Am only human.
We look at each other, the sky and I.
We understand each other, for

The solstice of summer has sagged, I stand
And wait. Virtue is rewarded, that
Is the nightmare, and I must tell you

That soon now, even before
The change from Daylight Saving Time, the sun,
Beyond the western ridge of black-burnt pine stubs like
A snaggery of rotten shark teeth, sinks
Lower, larger, more blank, and redder than
A mother's rage, as though
F.D.R. had never run for office even, or the first vagina
Had not had the texture of dream. Time

Is the mirror into which you stare.

Natural History

In the rain the naked old father is dancing, he will get wet.
The rain is sparse, but he cannot dodge all the drops.

He is singing a song, but the language is strange to me.

The mother is counting her money like mad, in the sunshine.
Like shuttles her fingers fly, and the sum is clearly astronomical.
Her breath is sweet as bruised violets, and her smile sways like daffodils
                                                    reflected in a brook.

The song of the father tells how at last he understands.
That is why the language is strange to me.

That is why clocks all over the continent have stopped.

The money the naked old mother counts is her golden memories of love.
That is why I see nothing in her maniacally busy fingers.

That is why all flights have been canceled out of Kennedy.

As much as I hate to, I must summon the police.
For their own good, as well as that of society, they must be put under
                                                    surveillance.

They must learn to stay in their graves. That is what graves are for.

Blow, West Wind

I know, I know—though the evidence
Is lost, and the last who might speak are dead.
Blow, west wind, blow, and the evidence, O,

Is lost, and wind shakes the cedar, and O,
I know how the kestrel hung over Wyoming,
Breast reddened in sunset, and O, the cedar

Shakes, and I know how cold
Was the sweat on my father's mouth, dead.
Blow, west wind, blow, shake the cedar, I know

How once I, a boy, crouching at creekside,
Watched, in the sunlight, a handful of water
Drip, drip, from my hand. The drops—they were bright!

But you believe nothing, with the evidence lost.

I Am Dreaming of a White Christmas:
The Natural History of a Vision

For Andrew Vincent Corry

[1]

No, not that door—never! But,
Entering, saw. Through
Air brown as an old daguerreotype fading. Through
Air that, though dust to the tongue, yet—
Like the inward, brown-glimmering twilight of water—
Swayed. Through brown air, dust-dry, saw. Saw
It.

   The bed.

      Where it had
Been. Now was. Of all
Covering stripped, the mattress
Bare but for old newspapers spread.
Curled edges. Yellow. On yellow paper dust,
The dust yellow. No! Do not.

         Do not lean to
Look at that date. Do not touch
That silken and yellow perfection of Time that
Dust is, for
There is no Time. I,
Entering, see.

    I,
Standing here, breathe the dry air.

[2]

        See
Yonder the old Morris chair bought soon
After marriage, for him to rest after work in, the leather,

Once black, now browning, brown at the dry cracks, streaked
With a fungoid green. Approaching,
See.

See it.

The big head. Propped,
Erect on the chair's leather pillow, bald skin
Tight on skull, not white now, brown
Like old leather lacquered, the big nose
Brown-lacquered, bold-jutting yet, but with
Nostril-flanges gone tattered. I have not
Yet looked at the eyes. Not
Yet.

The eyes
Are not there. But,
Not there, they stare at what
Is not there.

[3]

Not there, but
In each of the appropriate twin apertures, which are
Deep and dark as a thumb-gouge,
Something that might be taken for
A mulberry, large and black-ripe long back, but
Now, with years, dust-dried. The mulberries,
Desiccated, each out of
Its dark lurking-place, stare out at
Nothing.

His eyes
Had been blue.

[4]

Hers brown. But
Are not now. Now staring,
She sits in the accustomed rocker, but with
No motion. I cannot

181

Be sure what color the dress once was, but
Am sure that the fabric now falls decisively away
From the Time-sharpened angle of knees. The fabric
Over one knee, the left, has given way. And
I see what protrudes.

                    See it.

                    Above,
The dry fabric droops over breastlessness.

Over the shrouded femurs that now are the lap, the hands,
Palm-down, lie. The nail of one forefinger
Is missing.

               On the ring-finger of the left hand
There are two diamond rings. On that of the right,
One. On Sundays, and some evenings
When she sat with him, the diamonds would be on the fingers.

The rings. They shone.

Shine now.

In the brown air.

On the brown-lacquered face
There are now no
Lips to kiss with.

     [5]

The eyes had been brown. But
Now are not where eyes had been. What things
Now are where eyes had been but
Now are not, stare. At the place where now
Is not what once they
Had stared at.

There is no fire, on the cold hearth now,
To stare at.

182

[6]

        On
The ashes, gray, a piece of torn orange peel.
Foil wrappings of chocolates, silver and crimson and gold,
Yet gleaming from grayness. Torn Christmas paper,
Stamped green and red, holly and berries, not
Yet entirely consumed, but warped
And black-gnawed at edges. I feel

Nothing. A red
Ribbon, ripped long ago from some package of joy,
Winds over the gray hearth like
A fuse that failed. I feel
Nothing.

        Not even
When I see the tree.

Why had I not seen the tree before?
Why, on entering, had I not seen it?
It must have been there, and for
A long time, for
The boughs are, of all green, long since denuded.
That much is clear. For the floor
Is there carpeted thick with the brown detritus of cedar.

Christmas trees in our section were always cedar.

[7]

Beneath the un-greened and brown-spiked tree,
On the dead-fall of brown frond-needles, are,
I see, three packages. Identical in size and shape.
In bright Christmas paper. Each with red bow, and under
The ribbon, a sprig of holly.

        But look!

          The holly
Is, clearly, fresh.

*

I say to myself:

> *The holly is fresh.*

And
My breath comes short. For I am wondering
Which package is mine.

> *Oh, which?*

I have stepped across the hearth and my hand stretches out.

But the voice:

> *No presents, son, till the little ones come.*

[8]

What shadow of tongue, years back unfleshed, in what
Darkness locked in a rigid jaw, can lift and flex?

The man and the woman sit rigid. What had been
Eyes stare at the cold hearth, but I
Stare at the three chairs. Why—
Tell me why—had I not observed them before? For
They are here.

> The little red chair,
For the baby. The next biggest chair
For my little sister, the little red rocker. Then,
The biggest, my own, me the eldest.

The chairs are all empty.

> But
I am thinking a thought that is louder than words.
Thinking:

> *They're empty, they're empty, but me—oh, I'm here!*

*

And that thought is not words, but a roar like wind, or
The roar of the night-freight beating the rails of the trestle,
And you under the trestle, and the roar
Is nothing but darkness alive. Suddenly,
Silence.

       And no
Breath comes.

   [9]

        Where I was,
Am not. Now am
Where the blunt crowd thrusts, nudges, jerks, jostles,
And the eye is inimical. Then,
Of a sudden, know:

           Times Square, the season
Late summer and the hour sunset, with fumes
In throat and smog-glitter at sky-height, where
A jet, silver and ectoplasmic, spooks through
The sustaining light, which
Is yellow as acid. Sweat,
Cold in arm-pit, slides down flesh.

What year it is, I can't, for the life of me,
Guess, but know that,
Far off, south-eastward, in Bellevue,
In a bare room with windows barred, a woman,
Supine on an iron cot, legs spread, each ankle
Shackled to the cot-frame,
Screams.

She keeps on screaming because it is sunset.

Her hair has been hacked short.

[10]

Clerks now go home, night watchmen wake up, and the heart
Of the taxi-driver, just coming on shift,
Leaps with hope.

All is not in vain.

Old men come out from the hard-core movies.
They wish they had waited till later.

They stand on the pavement and stare up at the sky.
Their drawers are drying stiff at the crotch, and

The sky dies wide. The sky
Is far above the first hysteria of neon.

Soon they will want to go and get something to eat.

Meanwhile, down the big sluice of Broadway,
The steel logs jerk and plunge
Until caught in the rip, snarl, and eddy here before my face.

A mounted policeman sits a bay gelding. The rump
Of the animal gleams expensively. The policeman
Is some sort of dago. His jowls are swart.
His eyes are bright with seeing.

He is as beautiful as a law of chemistry.

[11]

In any case,
I stand here and think of snow falling. But am
Not here. Am
Otherwhere, for already,
This early and summer not over, in west Montana—
Or is it Idaho?—in
The Nez Perce Pass, tonight
It will be snowing.

*

186

The Nez Perce is more than 7,000 feet, and I
Have been there. The first flakes,
Large, soft, sparse, come straight down
And with enormous deliberation, white
Out of unbreathing blackness. Snow
Does not yet cling, but the tall stalk of bear-grass
Is pale in darkness. I have seen, long ago,
The paleness of bear-grass in darkness.

                                    But tell me, tell me,
Will I never know
What present there was in that package for me,
Under the Christmas tree?

    [12]

All items listed above belong in the world
In which all things are continuous,
And are parts of the original dream which
I am now trying to discover the logic of. This
Is the process whereby pain of the past in its pastness
May be converted into the future tense

Of joy.

Rattlesnake Country

For James Dickey

I

Arid that country and high, anger of sun on the mountains, but
One little patch of cool lawn:

                            Trucks
Had brought in rich loam. Stonework
Held it in place like a shelf, at one side backed
By the length of the house porch, at one end
By rock-fall. Above that, the mesquite, wolf-waiting. Its turn
Will, again, come.

                         Meanwhile, wicker chairs, all day,
Follow the shimmering shade of the lone cottonwood, the way that
Time, sadly seeking to know its own nature, follows
The shadow on a sun-dial. All day,
The sprinkler ejects its misty rainbow.

                            All day,
The sky shivers white with heat, the lake,
For its fifteen miles of distance, stretches
Tight under the white sky. It is stretched
Tight as a mystic drumhead. It glitters like neurosis.
You think it may scream, but nothing
Happens. Except that, bit by bit, the mountains
Get heavier all afternoon.

                         One day,
When some secret, high drift of air comes eastward over the lake,
Ash, gray, sifts minutely down on
Our lunch-time ice cream. Which is vanilla, and white.

There is a forest fire on Mount Ti-Po-Ki, which
Is at the western end of the lake.

2

If, after lunch, at God's hottest hour,
You make love, flesh, in that sweat-drench,
Slides on flesh slicker than grease. To grip
Is difficult.

       At drink-time,
The sun, over Ti-Po-Ki, sets
Lopsided, and redder than blood or bruised cinnabar, because of
The smoke there. Later,
If there is no moon, you can see the red eyes of fire
Wink at you from
The black mass that is the mountain.

At night, in the dark room, not able to sleep, you
May think of the red eyes of fire that
Are winking from blackness. You may,
As I once did, rise up and go from the house. But,
When I got out, the moon had emerged from cloud, and I
Entered the lake. Swam miles out,
Toward moonset. Motionless,
Awash, metaphysically undone in that silvered and
Unbreathing medium, and beyond
Prayer or desire, saw
The moon, slow, swag down, like an old woman's belly.

Going back to the house, I gave the now-dark lawn a wide berth.

At night the rattlers come out from the rock-fall.
They lie on the damp grass for coolness.

3

I-yee!—
       and the wranglers, they cry on the mountain, and waking
At dawn-streak, I hear it.

           High on the mountain
I hear it, for snow-water there, snow long gone, yet seeps down
To green the raw edges and enclaves of forest

189

With a thin pasturage. The wranglers
Are driving our horses down, long before daylight, plunging
Through gloom of the pines, and in their joy
Cry out:

     I-yee!

        We ride this morning, and,
Now fumbling in shadow for *levis*, pulling my boots on, I hear
That thin cry of joy from the mountain, and what once I have,
Literally, seen, I now in my mind see, as I
Will, years later, in my mind, see it—the horsemen
Plunge through the pine-gloom, leaping
The deadfall—*I-yee!*—
Leaping the boulder—*I-yee!*—and their faces
Flee flickering white through the shadow—*I-yee!*—
And before them,
Down the trail and in dimness, the riderless horses,
Like quicksilver spilled in dark glimmer and roil, go
Pouring downward.
        The wranglers cry out.

               And nearer.

                    But,
Before I go for my quick coffee-scald and to the corral,
I hear, much nearer, not far from my open window, a croupy
Gargle of laughter.

       It is Laughing Boy.

4

Laughing Boy is the name that my host—and friend—gives his yard-hand.
Laughing Boy is Indian, or half, and has a hare-lip.

Sometimes, before words come, he utters a sound like croupy laughter.
When he utters that sound his face twists. Hence the name.

Laughing Boy wakes up at dawn, for somebody
Has to make sure the rattlers are gone before

The nurse brings my host's twin baby daughters out to the lawn.
Laughing Boy, who does not like rattlers, keeps a tin can
Of gasoline covered with a saucer on an outer ledge of the porch.
Big kitchen matches are in the saucer. This
At the porch-end toward the rock-fall.

The idea is: Sneak soft-foot round the porch-end,
There between rattlers and rock-fall, and as one whips past,
Douse him. This with the left hand, and
At the same instant, with the nail of the right thumb,
Snap a match alight.

                    The flame,
If timing is good, should, just as he makes his rock-hole,
Hit him.

The flame makes a sudden, soft, gaspy sound at
The hole-mouth, then dances there. The flame
Is spectral in sunlight, but flickers blue at its raw edge.

Laughing Boy has beautiful coordination, and sometimes
He gets a rattler. You are sure if
The soft, gasping sound and pale flame come before
The stub-buttoned tail has disappeared.

                    Whenever
Laughing Boy really gets a rattler, he makes that sound like
Croupy laughter. His face twists.

Once I get one myself. I see, actually, the stub-buttoned tail
Whip through pale flame down into earth-darkness.

"The son-of-a-bitch," I am yelling, "did you see me, I got him!"

I have gotten that stub-tailed son-of-a-bitch.

I look up at the sky. Already, that early, the sky shivers with whiteness.

5

What was *is* is now *was*. But
Is *was* but a word for wisdom, its price? Some from
That long-lost summer are dead now, two of the girls then young,
Now after their pain and delusions, worthy endeavors and lies, are,
Long since, dead.

　　　　　The third
Committed her first adultery the next year, her first lover
A creature odd for her choosing, he who
Liked poetry and had no ambition, and
She cried out in his arms, a new experience for her. But
There were the twins, and she had, of course,
Grown accustomed to money.

　　　　　Her second,
A man of high social position, who kept a score-card. With her,
Not from passion this time, just snobbery. After that,
From boredom. Forgot, finally,
The whole business, took up horse-breeding, which
Filled her time and even, I heard, made unneeded money, and in
The old news photo I see her putting her mount to the jump.
Her yet beautiful figure is poised forward, bent elbows
Neat to her tight waist, face
Thrust into the cleansing wind of her passage, the face
Yet smooth as a girl's, no doubt from the scalpel
Of the plastic surgeon as well as
From her essential incapacity
For experience.

　　　　　The husband, my friend,
Would, by this time, be totally cynical. The children
Have been a disappointment. He would have heavy jowls.
Perhaps he is, by this time, dead.

As for Laughing Boy, he wound up in the pen. Twenty years.
This for murder. Indians
Just ought to leave whiskey to the white folks.

*

I can't remember the names of the others who came there,
The casual weekend-ers. But remember

What I remember, but do not
Know what it all means, unless the meaning inheres in
The compulsion to try to convert what now is *was*
Back into what was *is*.

                    I remember
The need to enter the night-lake and swim out toward
The distant moonset. Remember
The blue-tattered flick of white flame at the rock-hole
In the instant before I lifted up
My eyes to the high sky that shivered in its hot whiteness.

And sometimes—usually at dawn—I remember the cry on the mountain.

All I can do is to offer my testimony.

Homage to Theodore Dreiser: Psychological Profile

On the Centennial of His Birth (August 27, 1871)

> *Oh, the moon shines fair tonight along the Wabash,*
> *From the fields there comes the breath of new mown hay.*
> *Thro' the sycamores the candle lights are gleaming,*
> *On the banks of the Wabash, far away.*

> The Refrain of "On the Banks of the Wabash, Far Away"
> Words by Theodore Dreiser and Paul Dresser
> Music by Paul Dresser

Who is the ugly one slump-slopping down the street?
Who is the chinless wonder with the potato nose?
Can't you hear the soft *plop* of the pancake-shaped feet?

He floats, like Anchises' son, in the cloud of his fine new clothes,
Safe, safe at last, from the street's sneer, toward a queen who will fulfill
The fate devised him by Venus—but where, oh when! That is what he
never knows.

Born with one hand in his pants and one in the till,
He knows that the filth of self, to be loved, must be clad in glory,
So once stole twenty-five dollars to buy a new coat, and that is why still

The left eye keeps squinting backward—yes, history
Is gum-shoeing closer behind, with the constable-hand that clutches.
Watch his mouth, how it moves without sound, he is telling himself
his own old story.

Full of screaming his soul is, and a stench like live flesh that scorches.
It's the screaming, and stench, of a horse-barn aflame,
And the great beasts rear and utter, their manes flare up like torches.

From lies, masturbation, vainglory, and shame,
He moves in his dream of ladies swan-necked, with asses ample and sweet,
But knows that no kiss heals his soul, it is always the same.

The same—but a brass band plays in the distance, and the midnight cricket,
Though thinly, asseverates his name. He seeks amid the day's traffic a sign—
Some horseshoe or hunchback or pin—that now, at last, at the end of
this street

*

194

He will enter upon his reality: but enters only in-
To your gut, or your head, or your heart, to enhouse there and stay,
And in that hot darkness lie lolling and swell—like a tumor, perhaps benign.

May I present Mr. Dreiser? He will write a great novel, someday.

Stargazing

The stars are only a backdrop for
The human condition, the stars
Are brilliant above the black spruces,
And fall comes on. Wind

Does not move in the star-stillness, wind
Is afraid of itself, as you have been afraid in
Those moments when destruction and revelation
Have spat at each other like cats, and the mirror
Showed no breath, ha, ha, and the wind,

Far off in arctic starlight, is afraid
To breathe, and waits, huddled in
Sparse blackness of spruces, black glitter in starlight, in
A land, north, where snow already is, and waits:

And the girl is saying, "You do not look
At the stars," for I did not look at
The stars, for I know they are there, know
That if I look at the stars, I

Will have to live over again all I have lived
In the years I looked at stars and
Cried out, "O reality!" The stars
Love me. I love them. I wish they

Loved God, too. I truly wish that.

Little Boy and Lost Shoe

The little boy lost his shoe in the field.
Home he hobbled, not caring, with a stick whipping goldenrod.
Go find that shoe—I mean it, right now!
And he went, not now singing, and the field was big.

Under the sky he walked and the sky was big.
Sunlight touched the goldenrod, and yellowed his hair,
But the sun was low now, and oh, he should know
He must hurry to find that shoe, or the sun will be down.

Oh, hurry, boy, for the grass will be tall as a tree.
Hurry, for the moon has bled, but not like a heart, in pity.
Hurry, for time is money and the sun is low.
Yes, damn it, hurry, for shoes cost money, you know.

I don't know why you dawdle and do not hurry.
The mountains are leaning their heads together to watch.
How dilatory can a boy be, I ask you?

                            Off in Wyoming,
The mountains lean. They watch. They know.

There's a Grandfather's Clock in the Hall

There's a grandfather's clock in the hall, watch it closely. The minute
    hand stands still, then it jumps, and in between jumps there is
    no-Time,
And you are a child again watching the reflection of early morning
    sunlight on the ceiling above your bed,

Or perhaps you are fifteen feet under water and holding your breath as
    you struggle with a rock-snagged anchor, or holding your breath
    just long enough for one more long, slow thrust to make the orgasm
    really intolerable,
Or you are wondering why you really do not give a damn, as they trundle
    you off to the operating room,

Or your mother is standing up to get married and is very pretty, and
    excited and is a virgin, and your heart overflows, and you watch her
    with tears in your eyes, or
She is the one in the hospital room and she is really dying.

They have taken out her false teeth, which are now in a tumbler on the
    bedside table, and you know that only the undertaker will ever put
    them back in.
You stand there and wonder if you will ever have to wear false teeth.

She is lying on her back, and God, is she ugly, and
With gum-flabby lips and each word a special problem, she is asking if it is
    a new suit that you are wearing.

You say yes and hate her uremic guts, for she has no right to make you
    hurt the way that question hurts.
You do not know why that question makes your heart hurt like a kick in
    the scrotum,

*

For you do not yet know that the question, in its murderous triviality, is
    the last thing she will ever say to you,
Nor know what baptism is occurring in a sod-roofed hut or hole on the
    night-swept steppes of Asia, and a million mouths, like ruined stars in
    darkness, make a rejoicing that howls like wind, or wolves,

Nor do you know the truth, which is: *Seize the nettle of innocence in*
    both your hands, for this is the only way, and every
Ulcer in love's lazaret may, like a dawn-stung gem, sing—or even burst
    into whoops of, perhaps, holiness.

But, in any case, watch the clock closely. Hold your breath and wait.
Nothing happens, nothing happens, then suddenly, quick as a wink, and
    slick as a mink's prick, Time thrusts through the time of no-Time.

Reading Late at Night, Thermometer Falling

[I]

The radiator's last hiss and steam-clang done, he,
Under the bare hundred-watt bulb that glares
Like revelation, blanket
Over knees, woolly gray bathrobe over shoulders, handkerchief
On great bald skull spread, glasses
Low on big nose, sits. The book
Is propped on the blanket.

                    Thus—
But only in my mind's eye now:

                              and there, in the merciless
Glitter of starlight, the fields, mile
On mile over the county, stretch out and are
Crusted with ice which, whitely,
Answers the glitter of stars.

                    The mercury
Falls, the night is windless, mindless, and long, and somewhere,
Deep in the blackness of woods, the tendons
Of a massive oak bough snap with the sound of a
Pistol-shot.

          A beam,
Somewhere in the colding house where he sits,
Groans. But his eyes do not lift. Who,
Long back, had said to me:

"When I was young I felt like I
Had to try to understand how things are, before I died."

200

But lived long.

        Lived
Into that purity of being that may
Be had past all ambition and the frivolous hope, but who now
Lives only in my mind's eye,
            though I

Cannot see what book is propped there under that forever
Marching gaze—Hume's *History of England*, Roosevelt's
Winning of the West, a Greek reader,
Now Greek to him and held in his hands like a prayer, or
Some college text book, or Freud on dreams, abandoned
By one of the children. Or, even,
Coke or Blackstone, books forbidding and blackbound, and once I,
Perhaps twelve then, found an old photograph:

                      a young man,
In black coat, high collar, and string tie, black, one hand out
To lie with authority on a big book (Coke or Blackstone?), eyes
Lifted into space.

        And into the future.

               Which
Had not been the future. For the future
Was only his voice that, now sudden, said:

"Son, give me that!"

He took the photograph from my hand, said:

"Some kinds of foolishness a man is due to forget, son."

Tore it across. Tore
Time, and all that Time had been, across. Threw it
Into the fire. Who,
Years later, would say:

*

"I reckon I was lucky enough to learn early that a man can be happy
in his obligations."

Later, I found the poems. Not good.

[3]

The date on the photograph: 1890.

He was very young then. And poor.

Man lives by images. They
Lean at us from the world's wall, and Time's.

[4]

Night of the falling mercury, and ice-glitter.
Drouth-night of August and the horned insect booming
At the window-screen.

Ice-field, dusty road: distance flees.

And he sits there, and I think I hear
The faint click and grind of the brain as
It translates the perception of black marks on white paper into
Truth

Truth is all.

We must love it.

And he loved it, who once said:

"It is terrible for a man to live and not know."

Every day he walked out to the cemetery to honor his dead.
That was truth, too.

[5]

Dear Father—Sir—the "Sir" being
The sometimes disturbed recollection
Of the time when you were big, and not dead, and I
Was little, and all boys, of that time and place, automatically
Said that to their fathers, and to any other grown man,
White of course, or damned well got their blocks
Knocked off.

       So, Sir, I,
Who certainly could never have addressed you on a matter
As important as this when you were not dead, now
Address you on it for the last time, even though
Not being, after all my previous and sometimes desperate efforts,
Sure what a son can ever say to a father, even
A dead one.

       Indecipherable passion and compulsion—well,
Wouldn't it be sad to see them, of whatever
Dark root, dwindle into mere
Self-indulgence, habit, tic of the mind, or
The picking of a scab. Reality
Is hard enough to come by, but even
In its absence we need not blaspheme
It.

  Not that
You ever could, God knows. Though I,
No doubt, have, and even now
Run the risk of doing so when I say
That I live in a profound, though
Painful, gratitude to you for what
You could not help but be: i.e., yourself.

Who, aged eighty, said:

"I've failed in a lot of things, but I don't think anybody can say that
                        I didn't have guts."

Correct.

*

And I,
In spite of my own ignorance and failures,
Have forgiven you all your virtues.

                        Even your valor.

[6]

Who, aged eighty-six, fell to the floor,
Unconscious. Two days later,
Dead. Thus they discovered your precious secret:
A prostate big as a horse-apple. Cancer, of course.

No wonder you, who had not spent a day in bed,
Or uttered a single complaint, in the fifty years of my life,
Cried out at last.

You were entitled to that. It was only normal.

[7]

So disappeared.

                Simply not there.

                        And the seasons,
Nerve-tingling heat or premonitory chill, swung
Through the year, the years swung,

                            and the past, great
Eater of dreams, secrets, and random data, and
Refrigerator of truth, moved
Down what green valley at a glacier's
Massive pace,

            moving
At a pace not to be calculated by the trivial sun, but by
A clock more unforgiving that, at
Its distance of mathematical nightmare,

Glows forever. The ice-mass, scabbed
By earth, boulders, and some strange vegetation, moves
So imperceptibly that it seems
Only more landscape.

                Until,
In late-leveling light, some lunkhead clodhopper,
The clodhopper me,
The day's work done, now trudging home,
Stops.

    Stares.

       And there it is.

            It looms.

The bulk of the unnamable and de-timed beast is now visible,
Erect, in the thinly glimmering shadow of now sun-thinned ice.
                             Somehow yet
Alive.

                         The lunkhead
Stares.

      The beast,
From his preternatural height, unaware of
The cringe and jaw-dropped awe crouching there below, suddenly,
As if that shimmer of ice-screen had not even been there, lifts,

Into distance,

          the magisterial gaze.

  [8]

The mercury falls. Tonight snow is predicted. This,
However, is another country. Found in a common atlas.

Folly on Royal Street Before the Raw Face of God

Drunk, drunk, drunk, amid the blaze of noon,
Irrevocably drunk, total eclipse or,
At least, almost, and in New Orleans once,
In French Town, spring,
Off the Gulf, without storm warnings out,
Burst, like a hurricane of
Camellias, sperm, cat-squalls, fish-smells, and the old
Pain of fulfillment-that-is-not-fulfillment, so

Down Royal Street—Sunday and the street
Blank as my bank account
With two checks bounced—we—
C. and M. and I, every
Man-jack skunk-drunk—
Came.

       A cat,
Gray from the purple shadow of bougainvillaea,
Fish-head in dainty jaw-clench,
Flowed fluid as thought, secret as sin, across
The street. Was gone. We,
In the shock of that sudden and glittering vacancy, rocked
On our heels.

       A cop,
Of brachycephalic head and garlic breath,
Toothpick from side of mouth and pants ass-bagged and holster low,
From eyes the color of old coffee grounds,
Regarded with imperfect sympathy
La condition humaine—
Which was sure-God what we were.

We rocked on our heels.

*

At sky-height—
Whiteness ablaze in dazzle and frazzle of light like
A match flame in noon-glare—a gull
Kept screaming above the doomed city.
It screamed for justice against the face of God.

Raw-ringed with glory like an ulcer, God's
Raw face stared down.

And winked.

                                        We
Mouthed out our Milton for magnificence.

For what is man without magnificence?

Delusion, delusion!

                    But let
Bells ring in all the churches.
Let likker, like philosophy, roar
In the skull. Passion
Is all. Even
The sleaziest.

            War
Came. Among the bed-sheet Arabs, C.
Sported his gold oak leaf. Survived.
Got back. Back to the bank. But
One morning was not there. His books,
However, were in apple-pie order. His suits,
All dark, hung in the dark closet. Drawn up
In military precision, his black shoes,
Though highly polished, gave forth
No gleam in that darkness. In Mexico,
He died.

            For M.,
Twenty years in the Navy. Retired,
He fishes. Long before dawn, the launch slides out.

Land lost, he cuts the engine. The launch
Lifts, falls, in the time of the sea's slow breath.
Eastward, first light is like
A knife-edge honed to steel-brightness
And laid to the horizon. Sometimes,
He comes back in with no line wet.

As for the third, the tale
Is short. But long,
How long the art, and wisdom slow!—for him who
Once rocked on his heels, hearing the gull scream,
And quoted Milton amid the blaze of noon.

Birth of Love

Season late, day late, sun just down, and the sky
Cold gunmetal but with a wash of live rose, and she,
From water the color of sky except where
Her motion has fractured it to shivering splinters of silver,
Rises. Stands on the raw grass. Against
The new-curdling night of spruces, nakedness
Glimmers and, at bosom and flank, drips
With fluent silver. The man,

Some ten strokes out, but now hanging
Motionless in the gunmetal water, feet
Cold with the coldness of depth, all
History dissolving from him, is
Nothing but an eye. Is an eye only. Sees

The body that is marked by his use, and Time's,
Rise, and in the abrupt and unsustaining element of air,
Sway, lean, grapple the pond-bank. Sees
How, with that posture of female awkwardness that is,
And is the stab of, suddenly perceived grace, breasts bulge down in
The pure curve of their weight and buttocks
Moon up and, in that swelling unity,
Are silver, and glimmer. Then

The body is erect, she is herself, whatever
Self she may be, and with an end of the towel grasped in each hand,
Slowly draws it back and forth across back and buttocks, but
With face lifted toward the high sky, where
The over-wash of rose color now fails. Fails, though no star
Yet throbs there. The towel, forgotten,
Does not move now. The gaze
Remains fixed on the sky. The body,

*

Profiled against the darkness of spruces, seems
To draw to itself, and condense in its whiteness, what light
In the sky yet lingers or, from
The metallic and abstract severity of water, lifts. The body,
With the towel now trailing loose from one hand, is
A white stalk from which the face flowers gravely toward the high sky.
This moment is non-sequential and absolute, and admits
Of no definition, for it
Subsumes all other, and sequential, moments, by which
Definition might be possible. The woman,

Face yet raised, wraps,
With a motion as though standing in sleep,
The towel about her body, under the breasts, and,
Holding it there, hieratic as lost Egypt and erect,
Moves up the path that, stair-steep, winds
Into the clamber and tangle of growth. Beyond
The lattice of dusk-dripping leaves, whiteness
Dimly glimmers, goes. Glimmers and is gone, and the man,

Suspended in his darkling medium, stares
Upward where, though not visible, he knows
She moves, and in his heart he cries out that, if only
He had such strength, he would put his hand forth
And maintain it over her to guard, in all
Her out-goings and in-comings, from whatever
Inclemency of sky or slur of the world's weather
Might ever be. In his heart
He cries out. Above

Height of the spruce-night and heave of the far mountain, he sees
The first star pulse into being. It gleams there.

I do not know what promise it makes to him.

AUDUBON:
A VISION

Thou tellest my wanderings: put thou my tears
into thy bottle: are they not in thy book?

—Psalms 56:8

I caught at his strict shadow
and the shadow released itself
with neither haste nor anger.
But he remained silent.

—Carlos Drummond de Andrade:
"Travelling in the Family"
Translated by Elizabeth Bishop

Jean Jacques Audubon, whose name was anglicized when, in his youth, he was sent to America, was early instructed in the official version of his identity: that he was the son of the sea captain Jean Audubon and a first wife, who died shortly after his birth in Santo Domingo, and that the woman who brought him up in France was a second wife. Actually, he was the son of Jean Audubon and his mistress during the period when Jean Audubon was a merchant and slave-dealer in Santo Domingo, and the woman who raised him was the wife his father had left behind him in France while he was off making his fortune. By the age of ten Audubon knew the true story, but prompted, it would seem, by a variety of impulses, including some sound practical ones, he encouraged the other version, along with a number of flattering embellishments. He was, indeed, a fantasist of talent, but even without his help, legends accreted about him. The most famous one—that he was the lost Dauphin of France, the son of the feckless Louis XVI and Marie Antoinette—did not, in fact, enter the picture until after his death, in 1851.

I
Was Not the Lost Dauphin

[A]
Was not the lost dauphin, though handsome was only
Base-born and not even able
To make a decent living, was only
Himself, Jean Jacques, and his passion—what
Is man but his passion?

                    Saw,
Eastward and over the cypress swamp, the dawn,
Redder than meat, break;
And the large bird,
Long neck outthrust, wings crooked to scull air, moved
In a slow calligraphy, crank, flat, and black against
The color of God's blood spilt, as though
Pulled by a string.

                    Saw
It proceed across the inflamed distance.

Moccasins set in hoar frost, eyes fixed on the bird,
Thought: "On that sky it is black."
Thought: "In my mind it is white."
Thinking: "*Ardea occidentalis*, heron, the great one."

Dawn: his heart shook in the tension of the world.

Dawn: and what is your passion?

[B]
October: and the bear,
Daft in the honey-light, yawns.

The bear's tongue, pink as a baby's, out-crisps to the curled tip,
It bleeds the black blood of the blueberry.

*

213

The teeth are more importantly white
Than has ever been imagined.

The bear feels his own fat
Sweeten, like a drowse, deep to the bone.

Bemused, above the fume of ruined blueberries,
The last bee hums.

The wings, like mica, glint
In the sunlight.

He leans on his gun. Thinks
How thin is the membrane between himself and the world.

II
The Dream He Never Knew the End Of

[A]

Shank-end of day, spit of snow, the call,
A crow, sweet in distance, then sudden
The clearing: among stumps, ruined cornstalks yet standing, the spot
Like a wound rubbed raw in the vast pelt of the forest. There
Is the cabin, a huddle of logs with no calculation or craft:
The human filth, the human hope.

Smoke,
From the mud-and-stick chimney, in that air, greasily
Brims, cannot lift, bellies the ridgepole, ravels
White, thin, down the shakes, like sputum.

He stands,
Leans on his gun, stares at the smoke, thinks: "Punk-wood."
Thinks: "Dead-fall half-rotten." Too sloven,
That is, to even set axe to clean wood.

His foot,
On the trod mire by the door, crackles
The night-ice already there forming. His hand
Lifts, hangs. In imagination, his nostrils already
Know the stench of that lair beyond
The door-puncheons. The dog
Presses its head against his knee. The hand
Strikes wood. No answer. He halloos. Then the voice.

[B]

What should he recognize? The nameless face
In the dream of some pre-dawn cock-crow—about to say what,
Do what? The dregs
Of all nightmare are the same, and we call it
Life. He knows that much, being a man,
And knows that the dregs of all life are nightmare.

*

Unless.

Unless what?

   [C]
The face, in the air, hangs. Large,
Raw-hewn, strong-beaked, the haired mole
Near the nose, to the left, and the left side by firelight
Glazed red, the right in shadow, and under the tumble and tangle
Of dark hair on that head, and under the coarse eyebrows,
The eyes, dark, glint as from the unspecifiable
Darkness of a cave. It is a woman.

She is tall, taller than he.
Against the gray skirt, her hands hang.

"Ye wants to spend the night? Kin ye pay?
Well, mought as well stay then, done got one a-ready,
And leastwise, ye don't stink like no Injun."

   [D]
The Indian,
Hunched by the hearth, lifts his head, looks up, but
From one eye only, the other
An aperture below which blood and mucus hang, thickening slow.

"Yeah, a arrow jounced back off his bowstring.
Durn fool—and him a Injun." She laughs.

                        The Indian's head sinks.
So he turns, drops his pack in a corner on bearskin, props
The gun there. Comes back to the fire. Takes his watch out.
Draws it bright, on the thong-loop, from under his hunter's-frock.
It is gold, it lives in his hand in the firelight, and the woman's
Hand reaches out. She wants it. She hangs it about her neck.

And near it the great hands hover delicately
As though it might fall, they quiver like moth-wings, her eyes
Are fixed downward, as though in shyness, on that gleam, and her face
Is sweet in an outrage of sweetness, so that
His gut twists cold. He cannot bear what he sees.

*

Her body sways like a willow in spring wind. Like a girl.

The time comes to take back the watch. He takes it.
And as she, sullen and sunken, fixes the food, he becomes aware
That the live eye of the Indian is secretly on him, and soundlessly
The lips move, and when her back is turned, the Indian
Draws a finger, in delicious retardation, across his own throat.

After food, and scraps for his dog, he lies down:
In the corner, on bearskins, which are not well cured,
And stink, the gun by his side, primed and cocked.

Under his hand he feels the breathing of the dog.

The woman hulks by the fire. He hears the jug slosh.

   [E]
The sons come in from the night, two, and are
The sons she would have. Through slit lids
He watches. Thinks: "Now."

               The sons
Hunker down by the fire, block the firelight, cram food
Into their large mouths, where teeth
Grind in hot darkness, their breathing
Is heavy like sleep, he wants to sleep, but
The head of the woman leans at them. The heads
Are together in firelight.

He hears the jug slosh.

              Then hears,
Like the whisper and *whish* of silk, that other
Sound, like a sound of sleep, but he does not
Know what it is. Then knows, for,
Against firelight, he sees the face of the woman
Lean over, and the lips purse sweet as to bestow a kiss, but
This is not true, and the great glob of spit
Hangs there, glittering, before she lets it fall.

*

The spit is what softens like silk the passage of steel
On the fine-grained stone. It whispers.

When she rises, she will hold it in her hand.

　　[F]
With no sound, she rises. She holds it in her hand.
Behind her the sons rise like shadow. The Indian
Snores. Or pretends to.

　　　　　　　He thinks: "Now."

　　　　　　　　　　　　And knows

He has entered the tale, knows
He has entered the dark hovel
In the forest where trees have eyes, knows it is the tale
They told him when he was a child, knows it
Is the dream he had in childhood but never
Knew the end of, only
The scream.

　　[G]
But no scream now, and under his hand
The dog lies taut, waiting. And he, too, knows
What he must do, do soon, and therefore
Does not understand why now a lassitude
Sweetens his limbs, or why, even in this moment
Of fear—or is it fear?—the saliva
In his mouth tastes sweet.

"Now, now!" the voice in his head cries out, but
Everything seems far away, and small.

He cannot think what guilt unmans him, or
Why he should find the punishment so precious.

It is too late. Oh, oh, the world!

Tell me the name of the world.

[H]
The door bursts open, and the travelers enter:
Three men, alert, strong, armed. And the Indian
Is on his feet, pointing.

He thinks
That now he will never know the dream's ending.

[I]
Trussed up with thongs, all night they lie on the floor there.
The woman is gagged, for she had reviled them.
All night he hears the woman's difficult breath.

Dawn comes. It is gray. When he eats,
The cold corn pone grinds in his throat, like sand. It sticks there.

Even whiskey fails to remove it. It sticks there.

The leg-thongs are cut off the tied-ones. They are made to stand up.
The woman refuses the whiskey. Says: "What fer?"
The first son drinks. The other
Takes it into his mouth, but it will not go down.

The liquid drains, slow, from the slack of the mouth.

[J]
They stand there under the long, low bough of the great oak.
Eastward, low over the forest, the sun is nothing
But a circular blur of no irradiation, somewhat paler
Than the general grayness. Their legs
Are again bound with thongs.

They are asked if they want to pray now. But the woman:
"If'n it's God made folks, then who's to pray to?"
And then: "Or fer?" And bursts into laughing.

For a time it seems that she can never stop laughing.

But as for the sons, one prays, or tries to. And one
Merely blubbers. If the woman

Gives either a look, it is not
Pity, nor even contempt, only distance. She waits,

And is what she is,

And in the gray light of morning, he sees her face. Under
The tumbled darkness of hair, the face
Is white. Out of that whiteness
The dark eyes stare at nothing, or at
The nothingness that the gray sky, like Time, is, for
There is no Time, and the face
Is, he suddenly sees, beautiful as stone, and

So becomes aware that he is in the manly state.

    [K]
The affair was not tidy: bough low, no drop, with the clients
Simply hung up, feet not much clear of the ground, but not
Quite close enough to permit any dancing.
The affair was not quick: both sons long jerking and farting, but she,
From the first, without motion, frozen
In a rage of will, an ecstasy of iron, as though
This was the dream that, lifelong, she had dreamed toward.

                                              The face,
Eyes a-glare, jaws clenched, now glowing black with congestion
Like a plum, had achieved,
It seemed to him, a new dimension of beauty.

    [L]
There are tears in his eyes.
He tries to remember his childhood.
He tries to remember his wife.
He can remember nothing.

His throat is parched. His right hand,
Under the deerskin frock, has been clutching the gold watch.

The magic of that object had been,
In the secret order of the world, denied her who now hangs there.

*

220

He thinks: "What has been denied me?"
Thinks: "There is never an answer."

Thinks: "The question is the only answer."

He yearns to be able to frame a definition of joy.

    [M]
And so stood alone, for the travelers
Had disappeared into the forest and into
Whatever selves they were, and the Indian,
Now bearing the gift of a gun that had belonged to the hanged-ones,
Was long since gone, like smoke fading into the forest,
And below the blank and unforgiving eye-hole
The blood and mucus had long since dried.

He thought: "I must go."

                But could not, staring
At the face, and stood for a time even after
The first snowflakes, in idiotic benignity,
Had fallen. Far off, in the forest and falling snow,
A crow was calling..

              So stirs, knowing now
He will not be here when snow
Drifts into the open door of the cabin, or,
Descending the chimney, mantles thinly
Dead ashes on the hearth, nor when snow thatches
These heads with white, like wisdom, nor ever will he
Hear the infinitesimal stridor of the frozen rope
As wind shifts its burden, or when

The weight of the crow first comes to rest on a rigid shoulder.

III
We Are Only Ourselves

We never know what we have lost, or what we have found.
We are only ourselves, and that promise.
Continue to walk in the world. Yes, love it!

He continued to walk in the world.

IV
The Sign Whereby He Knew

[A]
His life, at the end, seemed—even the anguish—simple.
Simple, at least, in that it had to be.
Simply, what it was, as he was,
In the end, himself and not what
He had known he ought to be. The blessedness!—

To wake in some dawn and see,
As though down a rifle barrel, lined up
Like sights, the self that was, the self that is, and there,
Far off but in range, completing that alignment, your fate.

Hold your breath, let the trigger-squeeze be slow and steady.

The quarry lifts, in the halo of gold leaves, its noble head.

This is not a dimension of Time.

[B]
In this season the waters shrink.

The spring is circular and surrounded by gold leaves
Which are fallen from the beech tree.

Not even a skitter-bug disturbs the gloss
Of the surface tension. The sky

Is reflected below in absolute clarity.
If you stare into the water you may know

That nothing disturbs the infinite blue of the sky.

223

[C]
Keep store, dandle babies, and at night nuzzle
The hazelnut-shaped sweet tits of Lucy, and
With the piratical mark-up of the frontier, get rich.

But you did not, being of weak character.

You saw, from the forest pond, already dark, the great trumpeter swan
Rise, in clangor, and fight up the steep air where,
At the height of last light, it glimmered, like white flame.

The definition of love being, as we know, complex,
We may say that he, after all, loved his wife.

The letter, from campfire, keelboat, or slum room in New Orleans,
Always ended, "God bless you, dear Lucy." After sunset,

Alone, he played his flute in the forest.

[D]
Listen! Stand very still and,
Far off, where shadow
Is undappled, you may hear

The tusked boar grumble in his ivy-slick.

Afterward, there is silence until
The jay, sudden as conscience, calls.

The call, in the infinite sunlight, is like
The thrill of the taste of—on the tongue—brass.

[E]
The world declares itself. That voice
Is vaulted in—oh, arch on arch—redundancy of joy, its end
Is its beginning, necessity
Blooms like a rose. Why,

*

Therefore, is truth the only thing that cannot
Be spoken?
It can only be enacted, and that in dream,
Or in the dream become, as though unconsciously, action, and he stood,

At dusk, in the street of the raw settlement, and saw
The first lamp lit behind a window, and did not know
What he was. Thought: "I do not know my own name."

He walked in the world. He was sometimes seen to stand
In perfect stillness, when no leaf stirred.

Tell us, dear God—tell us the sign
Whereby we may know the time has come.

V
The Sound of That Wind

[A]
He walked in the world. Knew the lust of the eye.

Wrote: "Ever since a Boy I have had an astonishing desire
               to see Much of the World and particularly
               to acquire a true knowledge of the Birds of North America."

He dreamed of hunting with Boone, from imagination painted his portrait.
He proved that the buzzard does not scent its repast, but sights it.
He looked in the eye of the wounded white-headed eagle.

Wrote: ". . . the Noble Fellow looked at his Ennemies
               with a Contemptible Eye."

At dusk he stood on a bluff, and the bellowing of buffalo
Was like distant ocean. He saw
Bones whiten the plain in the hot daylight.

He saw the Indian, and felt the splendor of God.

Wrote: ". . . for there I see the Man Naked from his
               hand and yet free from acquired Sorrow."

Below the salt, in rich houses, he sat, and knew insult.
In the lobbies and couloirs of greatness he dangled,
And was not unacquainted with contumely.

Wrote: "My Lovely Miss Pirrie of Oackley Passed by Me
               this Morning, but did not remember how beautifull
               I had rendered her face once by Painting it
               at her Request with Pastelles."

Wrote: ". . . but thanks to My humble talents I can run
               the gantlet throu this World without her help."

*

226

And ran it, and ran undistracted by promise of ease,
Nor even the kind condescension of Daniel Webster.

Wrote: ". . . would give me a fat place was I willing to
        have one; but I love indepenn and piece more
        than humbug and money."

And proved same, but in the end, entered
On honor. Far, over the ocean, in the silken salons,
With hair worn long like a hunter's, eyes shining,
He whistled the bird-calls of his distant forest.

Wrote: ". . . in my sleep I continually dream of birds."

And in the end, entered into his earned house,
And slept in a bed, and with Lucy.

                    But the fiddle
Soon lay on the shelf untouched, the mouthpiece
Of the flute was dry, and his brushes.

                    His mind
Was darkened, and his last joy
Was in the lullaby they sang him, in Spanish, at sunset.

He died, and was mourned, who had loved the world.

Who had written: ". . . a world which though wicked enough
        in all conscience is *perhaps* as good
        as worlds unknown."

    [B]
So died in his bed, and
Night leaned, and now leans,
Off the Atlantic, and is on schedule.
Grass does not bend beneath that enormous weight
That with no sound sweeps westward. In the Mississippi,
On a mud bank, the wreck of a great tree, left
By flood, lies, the root-system and now-stubbed boughs
Lifting in darkness. It

Is white as bone. That whiteness
Is reflected in dark water, and a star
Thereby.

       Later,
In the shack of a sheep-herder, high above the Bitterroot,
The candle is blown out. No other
Light is visible.

The Northwest Orient plane, New York to Seattle, has passed,
                              winking westward.

   [C]
For everything there is a season.

But there is the dream
Of a season past all seasons.

In such a dream the wild-grape cluster,
High-hung, exposed in the gold light,
Unripening, ripens.

Stained, the lip with wetness gleams.

I see your lip, undrying, gleam in the bright wind.

I cannot hear the sound of that wind.

VI
Love and Knowledge

Their footless dance
Is of the beautiful liability of their nature.
Their eyes are round, boldly convex, bright as a jewel,
And merciless. They do not know
Compassion, and if they did,
We should not be worthy of it. They fly
In air that glitters like fluent crystal
And is hard as perfectly transparent iron, they cleave it
With no effort. They cry
In a tongue multitudinous, often like music.

He slew them, at surprising distances, with his gun.
Over a body held in his hand, his head was bowed low,
But not in grief.

He put them where they are, and there we see them:
In our imagination.

What is love?

One name for it is knowledge.

VII
Tell Me a Story

[A]
Long ago, in Kentucky, I, a boy, stood
By a dirt road, in first dark, and heard
The great geese hoot northward.

I could not see them, there being no moon
And the stars sparse. I heard them.

I did not know what was happening in my heart.

It was the season before the elderberry blooms,
Therefore they were going north.

The sound was passing northward.

[B]
Tell me a story.

In this century, and moment, of mania,
Tell me a story.

Make it a story of great distances, and starlight.

The name of the story will be Time,
But you must not pronounce its name.

Tell me a story of deep delight.

From

INCARNATIONS

Poems 1966-1968

Yet now our flesh is as the flesh of
our brethren . . .

—Nehemiah 5:5

John Henry said to the Captain,
"A man ain't nuthin but a man."

—Folk Ballad

Where the Slow Fig's Purple Sloth

Where the slow fig's purple sloth
Swells, I sit and meditate the
Nature of the soul, the fig exposes,
To the blaze of afternoon, one haunch
As purple-black as Africa, a single
Leaf the rest screens, but through it, light
Burns, and for the fig's bliss
The sun dies, the sun
Has died forever—far, oh far—
For the fig's bliss, thus.

                The air
Is motionless, and the fig,
Motionless in that imperial and blunt
Languor of glut, swells, and inward
The fibers relax like a sigh in that
Hot darkness, go soft, the air
Is gold.

     When you
Split the fig, you will see
Lifting from the coarse and purple seed, its
Flesh like flame, purer
Than blood.

       It fills
The darkening room with light.

Riddle in the Garden

My mind is intact, but the shapes
of the world change, the peach
has released the bough and at last
makes full confession, its *pudeur*
has departed like peach-fuzz wiped off, and

We now know how the hot sweet-
ness of flesh and the juice-dark hug
the rough peach-pit, we know its most
suicidal yearnings, it wants
to suffer extremely, it

Loves God, and I warn you, do not
touch that plum, it will burn you, a blister
will be on your finger, and you will
put the finger to your lips for relief—oh, do
be careful not to break that soft

Gray bulge of blister like fruit-skin, for
exposing that inwardness will
increase your pain, for you
are part of the world. You think
I am speaking in riddles. But I am not, for

The world means only itself.

The Red Mullet

The fig flames inward on the bough, and I,
Deep where the great mullet, red, lounges in
Black shadow of the shoal, have come. Where no light may

Come, he the great one, like flame, burns, and I
Have met him, eye to eye, the lower jaw horn,
Outthrust, arched down at the corners, merciless as

Genghis, motionless and mogul, and the eye of
The mullet is round, bulging, ringed like a target
In gold, vision is armor, he sees and does not

Forgive. The mullet has looked me in the eye, and forgiven
Nothing. At night I fear suffocation, is there
Enough air in the world for us all, therefore I

Swim much, dive deep to develop my lung-case, I am
Familiar with the agony of will in the deep place. Blood
Thickens as oxygen fails. Oh, mullet, thy flame

Burns in the shadow of the black shoal.

Masts at Dawn

Past second cock-crow yacht masts in the harbor go slowly white.

No light in the east yet, but the stars show a certain fatigue.
They withdraw into a new distance, have discovered our unworthiness.
                                                    It is long since

The owl, in the dark eucalyptus, dire and melodious, last called, and

Long since the moon sank and the English
Finished fornicating in their ketches. In the evening there was a
                                                    strong swell.

Red died the sun, but at dark wind rose easterly, white sea nagged the
                                        black harbor headland.

When there is a strong swell, you may, if you surrender to it, experience
A sense, in the act, of mystic unity with that rhythm. Your peace is
                                                    the sea's will.

But now no motion, the bay-face is glossy in darkness, like

An old window pane flat on black ground by the wall, near the ash
                                                    heap. It neither
Receives nor gives light. Now is the hour when the sea

Sinks into meditation. It doubts its own mission. The drowned cat
That on the evening swell had kept nudging the piles of the pier
                                                    and had seemed

To want to climb out and lick itself dry, now floats free. On that surface
                                        a slight convexity only, it is like

An eyelid, in darkness, closed. You must learn to accept the kiss of fate, for

*

236

The masts go white slow, as light, like dew, from darkness
Condensed on them, on oiled wood, on metal. Dew whitens in darkness.

I lie in my bed and think how, in darkness, the masts go white.

The sound of the engine of the first fishing dory dies seaward. Soon
In the inland glen wakes the dawn-dove. We must try

To love so well the world that we may believe, in the end, in God.

The Leaf

A

Here the fig lets down the leaf, the leaf
Of the fig five fingers has, the fingers
Are broad, spatulate, stupid,
Ill-formed, and innocent—but of a hand, and the hand,

To hide me from the blaze of the wide world, drops,
Shamefast, down. I am
What is to be concealed. I lurk
In the shadow of the fig. Stop.
Go no further. This is the place.

To this spot I bring my grief.
Human grief is the obscenity to be hidden by the leaf.

B

We have undergone ourselves, therefore
What more is to be done for Truth's sake? I

Have watched the deployment of ants, I
Have conferred with the flaming mullet in a deep place.

Near the nesting place of the hawk, among
Snag-rock, high on the cliff, I have seen
The clutter of annual bones, of hare, vole, bird, white
As chalk from sun and season, frail
As the dry grass stem. On that

High place of stone I have lain down, the sun
Beat, the small exacerbation
Of dry bones was what my back, shirtless and bare, knew. I saw

*

The hawk shudder in the high sky, he shudders
To hold position in the blazing wind, in relation to
The firmament, he shudders and the world is a metaphor, his eye
Sees, white, the flicker of hare-scut, the movement of vole.

Distance is nothing, there is no solution, I
Have opened my mouth to the wind of the world like wine, I wanted
To taste what the world is, wind dried up

The live saliva of my tongue, my tongue
Was like a dry leaf in my mouth.

Destiny is what you experience, that
Is its name and definition, and is your name, for

The wide world lets down the hand in shame:
Here is the human shadow, there, of the wide world, the flame.

     C
The world is fruitful, In this heat
The plum, black yet bough-bound, bursts, and the gold ooze is,
Of bees, joy, the gold ooze has striven
Outward, it wants again to be of
The goldness of air and—blessedly—innocent. The grape
Weakens at the juncture of the stem. The world

Is fruitful, and I, too,
In that I am the father
Of my father's father's father. I,
Of my father, have set the teeth on edge. But
By what grape? I have cried out in the night.

From a further garden, from the shade of another tree,
My father's voice, in the moment when the cicada ceases, has called to me.

     D
The voice blesses me for the only
Gift I have given: *teeth set on edge.*

*

In the momentary silence of the cicada,
I can hear the appalling speed,
In space beyond stars, of
Light. It is

A sound like wind.

From
TALE
OF TIME
Poems 1960-1966

Tale of Time

I. WHAT HAPPENED

It was October. It was the Depression. Money
Was tight. Hoover was not a bad
Man, and my mother
Died, and God
Kept on, and keeps on,
Trying to tie things together, but

It doesn't always work, and we put the body
Into the ground, dark
Fell soon, but not yet, and
Have you seen the last oak leaf of autumn, high,
Not yet fallen, stung
By last sun to a gold
Painful beyond the pain one can ordinarily
Get? What

Was there in the interim
To do, the time being the time
Between the clod's *chunk* and
The full realization, which commonly comes only after
Midnight? That

Is when you will go to the bathroom for a drink of water.
You wash your face in cold water.
You stare at your face in the mirror, wondering
Why now no tears come, for
You had been proud of your tears, and so
You think of copulation, of
Fluid ejected, of
Water deeper than daylight, of
The sun-dappled dark of deep woods and
Blood on green fern frond, of

243

The shedding of blood, and you will doubt
The significance of your own experience. Oh,
Desolation—oh, if
You were rich!
You try to think of a new position. Is this

Grief? You pray
To God that this be grief, for
You want to grieve.

This, you reflect, is no doubt the typical syndrome.

But all this will come later.
There will also be the dream of the eating of human flesh.

II. THE MAD DRUGGIST

I come back to try to remember the faces she saw every day.
She saw them on the street, at school, in the stores, at church.
They are not here now, they have been withdrawn, are put away,
They are all gone now, and have left me in the lurch.

I am in the lurch because they were part of her.
Not clearly remembering them, I have therefore lost that much
Of her, and if I do remember,
I remember the lineaments only beyond the ice-blur and soot-smutch

Of boyhood contempt, for I had not thought they were real.
The real began where the last concrete walk gave out
And the smart-weed crawled in the cracks, where the last privy canted
                                                            to spill
Over flat in the rank-nourished burdock, and would soon, no doubt,

If nobody came to prop it, which nobody would do.
The real began there: field and woods, stone and stream began
Their utterance, and the fox, in his earth, knew
Joy; and the hawk, like philosophy, hung without motion, high, where
                                                    the sun-blaze of wind ran.

*

244

Now, far from Kentucky, planes pass in the night, I hear them and all,
                                                                all is real.
Some men are mad, but I know that delusion may be one name for truth.
The faces I cannot remember lean at my bed-foot, and grin fit to kill,
For we now share a knowledge I did not have in my youth.

There's one I remember, the old druggist they carried away.
They put him in Hoptown, where he kept on making his list—
The same list he had on the street when he stopped my mother to say:
"Here they are, Miss Ruth, the folks that wouldn't be missed,

"Or this God-durn town would be lucky to miss,
If when I fixed a prescription I just happened to pour
Something in by way of improvement." Then leaned in that gray way
                                                                of his:
"But you—you always say something nice when you come in my store."

In Hoptown he worked on his list, which now could have nothing to do
With the schedule of deaths continuing relentlessly,
To include, in the end, my mother, as well as that list-maker who
Had the wit to see that she was too precious to die:

A fact some in the street had not grasped—nor the attending physician,
                                                                nor God, nor I.

III. ANSWER YES OR NO

Death is only a technical correction of the market.
Death is only the transfer of energy to a new form.
Death is only the fulfillment of a wish.

Whose wish?

IV. THE INTERIM

        I
Between the clod and the midnight
The time was.
There had been the public ritual and there would be
The private realization,
And now the time was, and

*

In that time the heart cries out for coherence.
Between the beginning and the end, we must learn
The nature of being, in order
In the end to *be*, so
Our feet, in first dusk, took
Us over the railroad tracks, where
Sole-leather ground drily against cinders, as when
Tears will not come. She

Whom we now sought was old. Was
Sick. Was dying. Was
Black. Was.
Was: and was that enough? Is
Existence the adequate and only target
For the total reverence of the heart?

We would see her who,
Also, had held me in her arms.
She had held me in her arms,
And I had cried out in the wide
Day-blaze of the world. But

Now was a time of endings.

What is love?

2

Tell me what love is, for
The harvest moon, gold, heaved
Over the far woods which were,
On the black land black, and it swagged over
The hill-line. That light
Lay gold on the roofs of Squiggtown, and the niggers
Were under the roofs, and
The room smelled of urine.
A fire burned on the hearth;
Too hot, and there was no ventilation, and

You have not answered my question.

3
Propped in a chair, lying down she
Could not have breathed, dying
Erect, breath
Slow from the hole of the mouth, that black
Aperture in the blackness which
Was her face, but
How few of them are really
Black, but she
Is black, and life

Spinning out, spilling out, from
The holes of the eyes: and the eyes are
Burning mud beneath a sky of nothing.
The eyes bubble like hot mud with the expulsion of vision.

I lean, I am the
Nothingness which she
Sees.

Her hand rises in the air.
It rises like revelation.
It moves but has no motion, and
Around it the world flows like a dream of drowning.
The hand touches my cheek.
The voice says: *you.*

I am myself.

The hand has brought me the gift of myself.

4
I am myself, and
Her face is black like cave-blackness, and over
That blackness now hangs death, gray
Like cobweb over the blackness of a cave, but
That blackness which she is, is
Not deficiency like cave-blackness, but is
Substance.
The cobweb shakes with the motion of her breath.

*

My hand reaches out to part that grayness of cobweb.

My lips touch the cheek, which is black.
I do not know whether the cheek is cold or hot, but I
Know that
The temperature is shocking.
I press my lips firmly against that death,
I try to pray.

The flesh is dry, and tastes of salt.

My father has laid a twenty-dollar bill on the table.
Secretly.
He, too, will kiss that cheek.

5
We stand in the street of Squiggtown.
The moon is high now and the tin roofs gleam.
My brother says: *The whole place smelled of urine.*
My father says: *Twenty dollars—oh, God, what*
Is twenty dollars when
The world is the world it is!

The night freight is passing.
The couplings clank in the moonlight, the locomotive
Labors on the grade.
The freight disappears beyond the coal chute westward, and
The red caboose light disappears into the distance of the continent.
It will move all night into distance.

My sister is weeping under the sky.
The sky is enormous in the absoluteness of moonlight.

These are factors to be considered in making any final estimate.

6
There is only one solution. If
You would know how to live, here
Is the solution, and under
My window, when ice breaks, the boulder now

248

Groans in the gorge, the foam swirls, and in
The intensity of the innermost darkness of steel
The crystal blooms like a star, and at
Dawn I have seen the delicate print of the coon-hand in silt by the riffle.

Hawk-shadow sweetly sweeps the grain.
I would compare it with that fugitive thought which I can find no
                                                          word for.

        7
Planes pass in the night. I turn
To the right side if the beating
Of my own heart disturbs me.
The sound of water flowing is
An image of Time, and therefore
Truth is all and
Must be respected, and
On the other side of the mirror into which,
At morning, you will stare, History

Gathers, condenses, crouches, breathes, waits. History
Stares forth at you through the eyes which
You think are the reflection of
Your own eyes in the mirror.
Ah, Monsieur du Miroir!

Your whole position must be reconsidered.

        8
But the solution: You
Must eat the dead.
You must eat them completely, bone, blood, flesh, gristle, even
Such hair as can be forced. You
Must undertake this in the dark of the moon, but
At your plenilune of anguish.

Immortality is not impossible,
Even joy.

249

V. WHAT WERE YOU THINKING, DEAR MOTHER?

What were you thinking, a child, when you lay,
At the whippoorwill hour, lost in the long grass,
As sun, beyond the dark cedars, sank?
You went to the house. The lamps were now lit.

What did you think when the mourning dove mourned,
Far off in those sober recesses of cedar?
What relevance did your heart find in that sound?
In lamplight, your father's head bent at his book.

What did you think when the last saffron
Of sunset faded beyond the dark cedars,
And on noble blue now the evening star hung?
You found it necessary to go to the house,

And found it necessary to live on,
In your bravery and in your joyous secret,
Into our present maniacal century,
In which you gave me birth, and in

Which I, in the public and private mania,
Have lived, but remember that once I,
A child, in the grass of that same spot, lay,
And the whippoorwill called, beyond the dark cedars.

VI. INSOMNIA

I

If to that place. Place of grass.
If to hour of whippoorwill, I.
If I now, not a child. To.
If now I, not a child, should come to
That place, lie in
That place, in that hour hear
That call, would
I rise,
Go?

*

250

Yes, enter the darkness. Of.
Darkness of cedars, thinking
You there, you having entered, sly,
My back being turned, face
Averted, or
Eyes shut, for
A man cannot keep his eyes steadily open
Sixty years.

I did not see you when you went away.

Darkness of cedars, yes, entering, but what
Face, what
Bubble on dark stream of Time, white
Glimmer un-mooned? Oh,
What age has the soul, what
Face does it wear, or would
I meet that face that last I saw on the pillow, pale?

I recall each item with remarkable precision.

Would the sweat now be dried on the temples?

  2
What would we talk about? The dead,
Do they know all, or nothing, and
If nothing, does
Curiosity survive the long unravelment? Tell me

What they think about love, for I
Know now at long last that the living remember the dead only
Because we cannot bear the thought that they
Might forget us. Or is
That true? Look, look at these—
But no, no light here penetrates by which
You might see these photographs I keep in my wallet. Anyway,
I shall try to tell you all that has happened to me.

Though how can I tell when I do not even know?

*

And as for you, and all the interesting things
That must have happened to you and that
I am just dying to hear about—

But would you confide in a balding stranger
The intimate secret of death?

3

Or does the soul have many faces, and would I,
Pacing the cold hypothesis of Time, enter
Those recesses to see, white,
Whiter than moth-wing, the child's face
Glimmer in cedar gloom, and so
Reach out that I might offer
What protection I could, saying,
"I am older than you will ever be"—for you
Are the child who once
Lay lost in the long grass, sun setting.

Reach out, saying: "Your hand—
Give it here, for it's dark and, my dear,
You should never have come in the woods when it's dark,
But I'll take you back home, they're waiting."
And to woods-edge we come, there I stand.

I watch you move across the open space.
You move under the paleness of new stars.
You move toward the house, and one instant,

A door opening, I see
Your small form black against the light, and the door
Is closed, and I

Hear night crash down a million stairs.
In the ensuing silence
My breath is difficult.

Heat lightning ranges beyond the horizon.

That, also, is worth mentioning.

4
Come,
Crack crust, striker
From darkness, and let seize—let what
Hand seize, oh!—my heart, and compress
The heart till, after pain, joy from it
Spurts like a grape, and I will grind
Teeth on flint tongue till
The flint screams. Truth
Is all. But

I must learn to speak it
Slowly, in a whisper.

Truth, in the end, can never be spoken aloud,
For the future is always unpredictable.
But so is the past, therefore

At wood's edge I stand, and,
Over the black horizon, heat lightning
Ripples the black sky. After
The lightning, as the eye
Adjusts to the new dark,
The stars are, again, born.

They are born one by one.

Elijah on Mount Carmel

To Vann and Glenn Woodward

(Elijah, after the miraculous fall of fire on his altar, the breaking of the drouth,
and the slaughter of the priests of Baal, girds up his loins and runs ahead of
the chariot of Ahab to the gates of Jezreel, where Jezebel waits.)

Nothing is re-enacted. Nothing
Is true. Therefore nothing
Must be believed,
But
To have truth
Something must be believed,
And repetition and congruence,
To say the least, are necessary, and
His thorn-scarred heels and toes with filth horn-scaled
Spurned now the flint-edge and with blood spurts flailed
Stone, splashed mud of Jezreel. And he screamed.
He had seen glory more blood-laced than any he had dreamed.

Far, far ahead of the chariot tire,
Which the black mud sucked, he screamed,
Screaming in glory
Like
A bursting blood blister.
Ahead of the mud-faltered fetlock,
He screamed, and of Ahab huddled in
The frail vehicle under the purpling wrack
And spilled gold of storm—poor Ahab, who,
From metaphysical confusion and lightning, had nothing to run to
But the soft Phoenician belly and commercial acuity
Of Jezebel: that darkness wherein History creeps to die.

How could he ever tell her? Get nerve to?
Tell how around her high altar
The prinking and primped
Priests,
Limping, had mewed,

*

And only the gull-mew was answer,
No fire to heaped meats, only sun-flame,
And the hairy one laughed: "Has your god turned aside to make pee-pee?"
How then on that sea-cliff he prayed, fire fell, sky darkened,
Rain fell, drouth broke now, for God had hearkened,
And priests gave their death-squeal. The king hid his eyes in his coat.
Oh, why to that hairy one should God have hearkened, who smelled
                                                                       like a goat?

Yes, how could he tell her? When he himself
Now scarcely believed it? Soon,
In the scented chamber,
She,
Saying, "Baby, Baby,
Just hush, now hush, it's all right,"
Would lean, reach out, lay a finger
To his lips to allay his infatuate gabble. So,
Eyes shut, breath scant, he heard her breath rip the lamp-flame
To blackness, and by that sweet dog-bait, lay, and it came,
The soft hand-grope he knew he could not, nor wished to, resist
Much longer. So prayed: "Dear God, dear God—oh, please, don't exist!"

Love: Two Vignettes

1. MEDITERRANEAN BEACH, DAY AFTER STORM

How instant joy, how clang
And whang the sun, how
Whoop the sea, and oh,
Sun, sing, as whiter than
Rage of snow, let sea the spume
Fling.

Let sea the spume, white, fling,
White on blue wild
With wind, let sun
Sing, while the world
Scuds, clouds boom and belly,
Creak like sails, whiter than,
Brighter than,
Spume in sun-song, oho!
The wind is bright.

Wind the heart winds
In constant coil, turning
In the—forever—light.

Give me your hand.

2. DECIDUOUS SPRING

Now, now, the world
All gabbles joy like geese, for
An idiot glory the sky
Bangs. Look!
All leaves are new, are
Now, are

Bangles dangling and
Spangling, in sudden air
Wangling, then
Hanging quiet, bright.

The world comes back, and again
Is gabbling, and yes,
Remarkably worse, for
The world is a whirl of
Green mirrors gone wild with
Deceit, and the world
Whirls green on a string, then
The leaves go quiet, wink
From their own shade, secretly.

Keep still, just a moment, leaves.

There is something I am trying to remember.

From
YOU, EMPERORS,
AND OTHERS

Poems 1957-1960

To Max and Carol Shulman

Tiberius on Capri

1

All is nothing, nothing all:
To tired Tiberius soft sang the sea thus,
Under his cliff-palace wall.
The sea, in soft approach and repulse,
Sings thus, and Tiberius,
Sea-sad, stares past the dusking sea-pulse
Yonder, where come,
One now by one, the lights, far off, of Surrentum.
He stares in the blue dusk-fall,
For all is nothing, nothing all.

Let darkness up from Asia tower.
On that darkening island behind him *spintriae* now stir.
In grot and scented bower,
They titter, yawn, paint lip, grease thigh,
And debate what role each would prefer
When they project for the Emperor's eye
Their expertise
Of his Eastern lusts and complex Egyptian fantasies.
But darkward he stares in that hour,
Blank now in totality of power.

2

There once, on that goat island, I,
As dark fell, stood and stared where Europe stank.
Many were soon to die—
From acedia snatched, from depravity, virtue,
Or frolic, not knowing the reason, in rank
On rank hurled, or in bed, or in church, or
Dishing up supper,
Or in a dark doorway, loosening the girl's elastic to tup her,
While high in the night sky,
The murderous tear dropped from God's eye;

*

And faintly forefeeling, forefearing, all
That to fulfill our time, and heart, would come,
I stood on the crumbling wall
Of that foul place, and my lungs drew in
Scent of dry gorse on the night air of autumn,
And I seized, in dark, a small stone from that ruin,
And I made outcry
At the paradox of powers that would grind us like grain, small and dry.
Dark down, the stone, in its fall,
Found the sea: I could do that much, after all.

Mortmain

AFTER NIGHT FLIGHT SON REACHES BEDSIDE OF
ALREADY UNCONSCIOUS FATHER, WHOSE RIGHT
HAND LIFTS IN A SPASMODIC GESTURE, AS
THOUGH TRYING TO MAKE CONTACT: 1955

In Time's concatenation and
Carnal conventicle, I,
Arriving, being flung through dark and
The abstract flight-grid of sky,
Saw rising from the sweated sheet and
Ruck of bedclothes ritualistically
Reordered by the paid hand
Of mercy—saw rising the hand—

Christ, start again! What was it I,
Standing there, travel-shaken, saw
Rising? What could it be that I,
Caught sudden in gut- or conscience-gnaw,
Saw rising out of the past, which I
Saw now as twisted bedclothes? Like law,
The hand rose cold from History
To claw at a star in the black sky,

But could not reach that far—oh, cannot!
And the star horribly burned, burns,
For in darkness the wax-white clutch could not
Reach it, and white hand on wrist-stem turns,
Lifts in last tension of tendon, but cannot
Make contact—*oh, oop-si-daisy*, churns
The sad heart, *oh, atta-boy, daddio's got*
One more shot in the locker, peas-porridge hot—

*

But no. Like an eyelid the hand sank, strove
Downward, and in that darkening roar,
All things—all joy and the hope that strove,
The failed exam, the admired endeavor,
Prizes and prinkings, and the truth that strove,
And back of the Capitol, boyhood's first whore—
Were snatched from me, and I could not move,
Naked in that black blast of his love.

Debate: Question, Quarry, Dream

Asking what, asking what?—all a boy's afternoon,
Squatting in the canebrake where the muskrat will come.
Muskrat, muskrat, please now, please, come soon.
He comes, stares, goes, lets the question resume.
He has taken whatever answer may be down to his mud-burrow gloom.

Seeking what, seeking what?—foot soft in cedar-shade.
Was that a deer-flag white past windfall and fern?
No, but by bluffside lurk powers and in the fern glade
Tall presences, standing all night, like white fox-fire burn.
The small fox lays his head in your hand now and weeps that you go,
                                                            not to return.

Dreaming what, dreaming what?—lying on the hill at twilight,
The still air stirred only by moth wing, the last stain of sun
Fading to moth-sky, blood-red to moth-white and starlight,
And Time leans down to kiss the heart's ambition,
While far away, before moonrise, come the town lights, one by one.

Long since that time I have walked night streets, heel-iron
Clicking the stone, and in dark in windows have stared.
Question, quarry, dream—I have vented my ire on
My own heart that, ignorant and untoward,
Yearns for an absolute that Time would, I thought, have prepared.

But has not yet. Well, let us debate
The issue. But under a tight roof, clutching a toy,
My son now sleeps, and when the hour grows late,
I shall go forth where the cold constellations deploy
And lift up my eyes to consider more strictly the appalling logic of joy.

From
PROMISES
Poems 1954-1956

To Rosanna and Gabriel

To a Little Girl, One Year Old, in a Ruined Fortress

To Rosanna

I. SIROCCO

To a place of ruined stone we brought you, and sea-reaches.
Rocca: fortress, hawk-heel, lion-paw, clamped on a hill.
A hill, no. On a sea cliff, and crag-cocked, the embrasures commanding
                                                    the beaches,
Range easy, with most fastidious mathematic and skill.

Philipus me fecit: he of Spain, the black-browed, the anguished,
For whom nothing prospered, though he loved God.
His arms, a great scutcheon of stone, once over the drawbridge,
                                                    have languished
Now long in the moat, under garbage; at moat-brink, rosemary with blue,
                                        thistle with gold bloom, nod.

Sun blaze and cloud tatter, now the sirocco, the dust swirl is swirled
Over the bay face, mounts air like gold gauze whirled; it traverses the
                                                    blaze-blue of water.
We have brought you where geometry of a military rigor survives its
                                                    own ruined world,
And sun regilds your gilt hair, in the midst of your laughter.

Rosemary, thistle, clutch stone. Far hangs Giannutri in blue air. Far to
                                        that blueness the heart aches,
And on the exposed approaches the last gold of gorse bloom, in the
                                                    sirocco, shakes.

II. THE CHILD NEXT DOOR

The child next door is defective because the mother,
Seven brats already in that purlieu of dirt,
Took a pill, or did something to herself she thought would not hurt,
But it did, and no good, for there came this monstrous other.

*

269

The sister is twelve. Is beautiful like a saint.
Sits with the monster all day, with pure love, calm eyes.
Has taught it a trick, to make *ciao*, Italian-wise.
It crooks hand in that greeting. She smiles her smile without taint.

I come, and her triptych beauty and joy stir hate
—Is it hate?—in my heart. Fool, doesn't she know that the process
Is not that joyous or simple, to bless, or unbless,
The malfeasance of nature or the filth of fate?

Can it bind or loose, that beauty in that kind,
Beauty of benediction? We must trust our hope to prevail
That heart-joy in beauty be wisdom, before beauty fail
And be gathered like air in the ruck of the world's wind!

I think of your goldness, of joy, but how empires grind, stars are hurled.
I smile stiff, saying *ciao*, saying *ciao*, and think: *This is the world.*

Infant Boy at Midcentury

1. WHEN THE CENTURY DRAGGED

When the century dragged, like a great wheel stuck at dead center;
When the wind that had hurled us our half-century sagged now,
And only velleity of air somewhat snidely nagged now,
With no certain commitment to compass, or quarter: then you chose
to enter.

You enter an age when the neurotic clock-tick
Of midnight competes with the heart's pulsed assurance of power.
You have entered our world at scarcely its finest hour,
And smile now life's gold Apollonian smile at a sick dialectic.

You enter at the hour when the dog returns to his vomit,
And fear's moonflower spreads, white as girl-thigh, in our dusk
of compromise;
When posing for pictures, arms linked, the same smile in their eyes,
Good and Evil, to iron out all differences, stage their meeting at summit.

You come in the year when promises are broken,
And petal fears the late, as fruit the early frost-fall;
When the young expect little, and the old endure total recall,
But discover no logic to justify what they had taken, or forsaken.

But to take and forsake now you're here, and the heart will compress
Like stone when we see that rosy heel learn,
With its first step, the apocalyptic power to spurn
Us, and our works and days, and onward, prevailing, pass

To pause, in high pride of unillusioned manhood,
At the gap that gives on the new century, and land,
And with calm heart and level eye command
That dawning perspective and possibility of human good.

You will read the official histories—some true, no doubt.
Barring total disaster, the record will speak from the shelf.
And if there's disaster, disaster will speak for itself.
So all of our lies will be truth, and the truth vindictively out.

Remember our defects, we give them to you gratis.
But remember that ours is not the worst of times.
Our country's convicted of follies rather than crimes—
We throw out baby with bath, drop the meat in the fire where the fat is.

And in even such stew and stink as Tacitus
Once wrote of, his generals, gourmets, pimps, poltroons,
He found persons of private virtue, the old-fashioned stout ones
Who would bow the head to no blast; and we know that such are yet
                                                              with us.

He was puzzled how virtue found perch past confusion and wrath;
How even Praetorian brutes, blank of love, as of hate,
Proud in their craftsman's pride only, held a last gate,
And died, each back unmarred as though at the barracks bath.

And remember that many among us wish you well;
And once, on a strange shore, an old man, toothless and through,
Groped a hand from the lattice of personal disaster to touch you.
He sat on the sand for an hour; said *ciao, bello*, as evening fell.

And think, as you move past our age that grudges and grieves,
How eyes, purged of envy, will follow your sunlit chance.
Eyes will brighten to follow your brightness and dwindle of distance.
From privacy of fate, eyes will follow, as though from the shadow
                                                              of leaves.

Man in Moonlight

MOONLIGHT OBSERVED FROM RUINED FORTRESS

Great moon, white-westering past our battlement,
Dark sea offers silver scintillance to your sky,
And not less responsive would my human heart be if I
Had been duly instructed in what such splendors have meant.

I have thought on the question by other sea, other shore:
When you smoothed the sweet Gulf asleep, like a babe at the breast.
When the moon-lashed old freighter banged stars in Atlantic unrest.
When you spangled spume-tangle on black rock, and seals barked
                                                    at sea-roar.

Décor must be right, of course, for your massive effect,
But a Tennessee stock-pond is not beneath your contempt,
Though its littoral merely a barnyard with cow-pats, unkempt.
Yes, to even a puddle you've been known to pay some respect.

And once on the Cumberland's bluffs I stood at midnight,
With music and laughter behind me, while my eyes
Were trapped in gleam-glory, but the heart's hungry surmise
Faded. So back to the racket and bottle's delight.

Be it sea or a sewer, we know you have never much cared
What sort of excuse, just so you may preen and prink,
With vulgarities to make Belasco blink
And tricks that even Houdini wouldn't have dared.

So now with that old, anguishing virtuosity
You strike our cliff, and then lean on to Carthage.
We stand on the crumbling stone and ruins of rage,
To watch your Tyrrhenian silver prank the sea.

*

273

And so we enact again the compulsive story,
Knowing of course the end—and ah, how soon—
But caught in that protocol of plenilune
And our own werewolf thirst to drink the blood of glory.

We stare, we stare, but will not stare for long.
You will not tell us what we need to know.
Our feet soon go the way that they must go,
In diurnal dust and heat, and right and wrong.

Dragon Country: To Jacob Boehme

This is the dragon's country, and these his own streams.
The slime on the railroad rails is where he has crossed the track.
On a frosty morning, that field mist is where his great turd steams,
And there are those who have gone forth and not come back.

I was only a boy when Jack Simms reported the first depredation,
What something had done to his hog pen. They called him a
                                        God-damn liar.
Then said it must be a bear, after some had viewed the location,
With fence rails, like matchwood, splintered, and earth a bloody mire.

But no bear had been seen in the county in fifty years, they knew.
It was something to say, merely that, for people compelled to explain
What, standing in natural daylight, they couldn't believe to be true;
And saying the words, one felt in the chest a constrictive pain.

At least, some admitted this later, when things had got to the worst—
When, for instance, they found in the woods the wagon turned on its side,
Mules torn from trace chains, and you saw how the harness had burst.
Spectators averted the face from the spot where the teamster had died.

But that was long back, in my youth, just the first of case after case.
The great hunts fizzled. You followed the track of disrepair,
Ruined fence, blood-smear, brush broken, but came in the end to a place
With weed unbent and leaf calm—and nothing, nothing, was there.

So what, in God's name, could men think when they couldn't bring to bay
That belly-dragging earth-evil, but found that it took to air?
Thirty-thirty or buckshot might fail, but then at least you could say
You had faced it—assuming, of course, that you had survived the affair.

We were promised troops, the Guard, but the Governor's skin got thin
When up in New York the papers called him Saint George of Kentucky.
Yes, even the Louisville reporters who came to Todd County would grin.
Reporters, though rarely, still come. No one talks. They think it unlucky.

*

If a man disappears—well, the fact is something to hide.
The family says, gone to Akron, or up to Ford, in Detroit.
When we found Jebb Johnson's boot, with the leg, what was left, inside,
His mother said, no, it's not his. So we took it out to destroy it.

Land values are falling, no longer do lovers in moonlight go.
The rabbit, thoughtless of air gun, in the nearest pasture cavorts.
Now certain fields go untended, the local birth rate goes low.
The coon dips his little black paw in the riffle where he nightly resorts.

Yes, other sections have problems somewhat different from ours.
Their crops may fail, bank rates rise, loans at rumor of war be called,
But we feel removed from maneuvers of Russia, or other great powers,
And from much ordinary hope we are now disenthralled.

The Catholics have sent in a mission, Baptists report new attendance.
But all that's off the point! We are human, and the human heart
Demands language for reality that has not the slightest dependence
On desire, or need—and in church fools pray only that the Beast depart.

But if the Beast were withdrawn now, life might dwindle again
To the ennui, the pleasure, and the night sweat, known in the time before
Necessity of truth had trodden the land, and our hearts, to pain,
And left, in darkness, the fearful glimmer of joy, like a spoor.

Lullaby: Smile in Sleep

Sleep, my son, and smile in sleep.
You will dream the world anew.
Watching you now sleep,
I feel the world's depleted force renew,
Feel the nerve expand and knit,
Feel a rustle in the blood,
Feel wink of warmth and stir of spirit,
As though spring woke in the heart's cold underwood.
The vernal work is now begun.
Sleep, my son.
Sleep, son.

You will see the nestling fall.
Blood flecks grass of the rabbit form.
You will, of course, see all
The world's brute ox-heel wrong, and shrewd hand-harm.
Throats are soft to invite the blade.
Truth invites the journalist's lie.
Love bestowed mourns trust betrayed,
But the heart most mourns its own infidelity.
The greater, then, your obligation.
Dream perfection.
Dream, son.

When the diver leaves the board
To hang at gleam-height against the sky,
Trajectory is toward
An image hung perfect as light in his mind's wide eye.
So your dream will later serve you.
So now, dreaming, you serve me,
And give our hope new patent to
Enfranchise human possibility.
Grace undreamed is grace forgone.
Dream grace, son.
Sleep on.

*

Dream that sleep is a sunlit meadow
Drowsy with a dream of bees
Threading sun, and a shadow
Where you may lie lulled by their sunlit industries.
Let the murmurous bees of sleep
Tread down honey in the honeycomb.
Heart-deep now, your dream will keep
Sweet in that deep comb for time to come.
Dream the sweetness coming on.
Dream, sweet son.
Sleep on.

What if angry vectors veer
Around your sleeping head, and form?
There's never need to fear
Violence of the poor world's abstract storm.
For now you dream Reality.
Matter groans to touch your hand.
Matter lifts now like the sea
Toward that strong moon that is your dream's command.
Dream the power coming on.
Dream, strong son.
Sleep on.

Lullaby: A Motion Like Sleep

Under the star and beech-shade braiding,
Past the willow's dim solicitudes,
Past hush of oak-dark and a stone's star-glinted upbraiding,
Water moves, in a motion like sleep,
Along the dark edge of the woods.
So, son, now sleep.

Sleep, and feel how now, at woods-edge,
The water, wan, moves under starlight,
Before it finds that dark of its own deepest knowledge,
And will murmur, in motion like sleep,
In that leaf-dark languor of night.
So, son, sleep deep.

Sleep, and dream how deep and dreamless
The covered courses of blood are:
And blood, in a motion like sleep, moves, gleamless,
By alleys darkened deep now
In the leafage of no star.
So, son, sleep now.

Sleep, for sleep and stream and blood-course
Are a motion with one name,
And all that flows finds end but in its own source,
And a circuit of motion like sleep,
And will go as once it came.
So, son, now sleep

Till the clang of cock-crow, and dawn's rays,
Summon your heart and hand to deploy
Their energies to know, in the excitement of day-blaze,
How like a wound, and deep,
Is Time's irremediable joy.
So, son, now sleep.

279

School Lesson Based on Word of Tragic Death of Entire Gillum Family

They weren't so bright, or clean, or clever,
    And their noses were sometimes imperfectly blown,
But they always got to school the weather whatever,
    With old lard pail full of fried pie, smoked ham, and corn pone.

Tow hair was thick s a corn-shuck mat.
    They had milky blue eyes in matching pairs,
And barefoot or brogan, when they sat,
    Their toes were the kind that hook round the legs of chairs.

They had adenoids to make you choke,
    And buttermilk breath, and their flannels asteam,
And sat right mannerly while teacher spoke,
    But when book-time came their eyes were glazed and adream.

There was Dollie-May, Susie-May, Forrest, Sam, Brother—
    Thirteen down to eight the stairsteps ran.
They had popped right natural from their big fat mother—
    The clabber kind that can catch just by honing after a man.

In town, Gillum stopped you, he'd say: "Say, mister,
    I'll name you what's true fer folks, ever-one.
Human-man ain't much mo, 'n a big blood blister.
    All red and proud-swole, but one good squeeze and he's gone.

"Take me, ain't wuth lead and powder to perish,
    Just some spindle bone stuck in a pair of pants,
But a man's got his chaps to love and to cherish,
    And raise up and larn 'em so they kin git they chance."

So mud to the hub, or dust to the hock,
    God his helper, wet or dry,
Old Gillum swore by God and by cock,
    He'd git 'em larned before his own time came to die.

*

280

That morning blew up cold and wet,
    All the red-clay road was curdled as curd,
And no Gillums there for the first time yet.
    The morning drones on. Stove spits. Recess. Then the word.

Dollie-May was combing Susie-May's head.
    Sam was feeding, Forrest milking, got nigh through.
Little Brother just sat on the edge of his bed.
    Somebody must have said: "Pappy, now what you aimin' to do?"

An ice pick is a subtle thing.
    The puncture's small, blood only a wisp.
It hurts no more than a bad bee sting.
    When the sheriff got there the school-bread was long burned to a crisp.

In the afternoon silence the chalk would scrape.
    We sat and watched the windowpanes steam,
Blur the old corn field and accustomed landscape.
    Voices came now faint in our intellectual dream.

Which shoe—yes, which—was Brother putting on?
    That was something, it seemed, you just had to know.
But nobody knew, all afternoon,
    Though we studied and studied, as hard as we could, to know,

Studying the arithmetic of losses,
    To be prepared when the next one,
By fire, flood, foe, cancer, thrombosis,
    Or Time's slow malediction, came to be undone.

We studied all afternoon, till getting on to sun.
There would be another lesson, but we were too young to take up that one.

Founding Fathers, Early-Nineteenth-Century Style, Southeast U.S.A.

They were human, they suffered, wore long black coat and gold
watch chain.
They stare from daguerreotype with severe reprehension,
Or from genuine oil, and you'd never guess any pain
In those merciless eyes that now remark our own time's sad declension.

Some composed declarations, remembering Jefferson's language.
Knew pose of the patriot, left hand in crook of the spine or
With finger to table, while right invokes the Lord's just rage.
There was always a grandpa, or cousin at least, who had been a real Signer.

Some were given to study, read Greek in the forest, and these
Longed for an epic to do their own deeds right honor;
Were Nestor by pigpen, in some tavern brawl played Achilles.
In the ring of Sam Houston they found, when he died, one word
engraved: *Honor.*

Their children were broadcast, like millet seed flung in a wind-flare.
Wives died, were dropped like old shirts in some corner of country.
Said, "Mister," in bed, the child-bride; hadn't known what to find there;
Wept all the next morning for shame; took pleasure in silk; wore the
keys to the pantry.

"Will die in these ditches if need be," wrote Bowie, at the Alamo.
And did, he whose left foot, soft-catting, came forward, and breath hissed:
Head back, gray eyes narrow, thumb flat along knife-blade, blade low.
"Great gentleman," said Henry Clay, "and a patriot." Portrait by
Benjamin West.

Or take those, the nameless, of whom no portraits remain,
No locket or seal ring, though somewhere, broken and rusted,
In attic or earth, the long Decherd, stock rotten, has lain;
Or the mold-yellow Bible, God's Word, in which, in their strength,
they also trusted.

*

Some wrestled the angel, and took a fall by the corncrib.
Fought the brute, stomp-and-gouge, but knew they were doomed in
                                                 that glory.
All night, in sweat, groaned; fell at last with spit red and a cracked rib.
How sweet then the tears! Thus gentled, they roved the dark land with
                                                the old story.

Some prospered, had black men and acres, and silver on table,
But remembered the owl call, the smell of burnt bear fat on dusk-air.
Loved family and friends, and stood it as long as able—
"But money and women, too much is ruination, am Arkansas-bound."
                                                 So went there.

One of mine was a land shark, or so the book with scant praise
Denominates him. "A man large and shapeless,
Like a sack of potatoes set on a saddle," it says,
"Little learning but shrewd, not well trusted." Rides thus out of history,
                                               neck fat and napeless.

One fought Shiloh and such, got cranky, would fiddle all night.
The boys nagged for Texas. "God damn it, there's nothing, God damn it,
In Texas"—but took wagons, went, and to prove he was right,
Stayed a year and a day—"hell, nothing in Texas"—had proved it, came
                                             back to black vomit,

And died, and they died, and are dead, and now their voices
Come thin, like the last cricket in frost-dark, in grass lost,
With nothing to tell us for our complexity of choices,
But beg us only one word to justify their own old life-cost.

So let us bend ear to them in this hour of lateness,
And what they are trying to say, try to understand,
And try to forgive them their defects, even their greatness,
For we are their children in the light of humanness, and under the
                                           shadow of God's closing hand.

From

SELECTED
POEMS
1923-1943

The Ballad of Billie Potts

(When I was a child I heard this story from an old lady who was a relative of mine. The scene, according to her version, was in the section of Western Kentucky known as "Between the Rivers," the region between the Cumberland and the Tennessee. The name of Bardstown in the present account refers to Bardstown, Kentucky, where, it is said, the first race track west of the mountains was laid out late in the eighteenth century.)

Big Billie Potts was big and stout
In the land between the rivers
His shoulders were wide and his gut stuck out
Like a croker of nubbins and his holler and shout
Made the bob-cat shiver and the black-jack leaves shake
In the section between the rivers.
He would slap you on your back and laugh.

Bib Billie had a wife, she was dark and little
In the land between the rivers,
And clever with her wheel and clever with her kettle,
But she never said a word and when she sat
By the fire her eyes worked slow and narrow like a cat.
Nobody knew what was in her head.

They had a big boy with fuzz on his chin
So tall he ducked the door when he came in,
A clabber-headed bastard with snot in his nose
And big red wrists hanging out of his clothes
And a whicker when he laughed where his father had a bellow
In the section between the rivers.
They called him Little Billie.
He was their darling.

(It is not hard to see the land, what it was.
Low hills and oak. The fetid bottoms where
The slough uncoils, and in the tangled cane,
Where no sun comes, the muskrat's astute face
Is lifted to the yammering jay; then dropped.
A cabin where the shagbark stood and the
Magnificent tulip-tree; both now are gone.
But the land is there, and as you top a rise,

Beyond you all the landscape steams and simmers
—The hills, now gutted, red, cane-brake and black-jack yet.

The oak leaf steams under the powerful sun.
"Mister, is this the right road to Paducah?"
The red face, seamed and gutted like the hill,
Slow under time, and with the innocent savagery
Of Time, the bleared eyes rolling, answers from
Your dream: "They names hit so, but I ain't bin.")

Big Billie was the kind who laughed but could spy
The place for a ferry where folks would come by.
He built an inn and folks bound West
Hitched their horses there to take their rest
And grease the gall and grease the belly
And jaw and spit under the trees
In the section between the rivers.
Big Billie said: "Git down, friend, and take yore ease!"
He would slap you on your back and set you at his table.

(Leaning and slow, you see them move
In massive passion colder than any love:
Their lips move but you do not hear the words,
Nor trodden twig nor fluted irony of birds,
Nor hear the rustle of the heart
That, heave and settle, gasp and start,
Heaves like a fish in the ribs' dark basket borne
West from the great water's depth whence it was torn.

Their names are like the leaves, but are forgot
—The slush and swill of the world's great pot
That foamed at the Appalachian lip, and spilled
Like quicksilver across green baize, the unfulfilled
Disparate glitter, gleam, wild symptom, seed
Flung in the long wind: silent, they proceed
Past meadow, salt-lick, and the lyric swale;
Enter the arbor, shadow of trees, fade, fail.)

Big Billie was sharp at swap and trade
And could smell the nest where the egg was laid.
He could read and cipher and they called him squire,

And he added up his money while he sat by the fire,
And sat in the shade while folks sweated and strove,
For he was the one who fatted and throve
In the section between the rivers.
"Thank you kindly, sir," Big Billie would say
When the man in the black coat paid him at streak of day
And swung to the saddle, was ready to go,
And rode away and didn't know
That he was already as good as dead,
For at midnight the message had been sent ahead:
"Man in black coat, riding bay mare with star."

(There was a beginning but you cannot see it.
There will be an end but you cannot see it.
They will not turn their faces to you though you call,
Who pace a logic merciless as light,
Whose law is their long shadow on the grass,
Sun at the back; who pace, pass,
And passing nod in that glacial delirium
While the tight sky shudders like a drum
And speculation rasps its idiot nails
Across the dry slate where you did the sum.

The answer is in the back of the book but the page is gone.
And Grandma told you to tell the truth, but she is dead.
And heedless, their hairy faces fixed
Beyond your call or question now, they move
Under the infatuate weight of their wisdom,
Precious but for the preciousness of their burden,
Sainted and sad and sage as the hairy ass, these who bear
History like bound faggots, with stiff knees;
And breathe the immaculate climate where
The lucent leaf is lifted, lank beard fingered, by no breeze,
Rapt in the fabulous complacency of fresco, vase, or frieze:

And the testicles of the fathers hang down like old lace.)

Little Billie was full of vinegar
And full of sap as a maple tree
And full of tricks as a lop-eared pup,
So one night when the runner didn't show up,

Big Billie called Little and said, "Saddle up,"
And nodded toward the man who was taking his sup
With his belt unlatched and his feet to the fire.
Big Billie said, "Give Amos a try.
Fer this feller takes the South Fork and Amos'll be nigher
Than Badly or Buster, and Amos is sly
And slick as a varmint, and I don't deny
I lak business with Amos, fer he's one you kin trust
In the section between the rivers,
And it looks lak they's mighty few.
Amos will split up fair and square."

Little Billie had something in his clabber-head
By way of brains, and he reckoned he knew
How to skin a cat or add two and two.
So long before the sky got red
Over the land between the rivers,
He hobbled his horse back in the swamp
And squatted on his hams in the morning dew and damp
And scratched his stomach and grinned to think
How Pap would be proud and Mammy glad
To know what a thriving boy they had.
He always was a good boy to his darling Mammy.

(Think of yourself riding away from the dawn,
Think of yourself and the unnamed ones who had gone
Before, riding, who rode away from *goodbye, goodbye,*
And toward *hello,* toward Time's unwinking eye;
And like the cicada had left, at cross-roads or square,
The old shell of self, thin, ghostly, translucent, light as air;
At dawn riding into the curtain of unwhispering green,
Away from the vigils and voices into the green
World, land of the innocent bough, land of the leaf.
Think of your own face green in the submarine light of the leaf.

Or think of yourself crouched at the swamp-edge:
Dawn-silence past last owl-hoot and not yet at day-verge
First bird-stir, titmouse or drowsy warbler not yet.
You touch the grass in the dark and your hand is wet.
Then light: and you wait for the stranger's hoofs on the soft trace,
And under the green leaf's translucence the light bathes your face.

*

Think of yourself at dawn: Which one are you? What?)

Little Billie heard hoofs on the soft grass,
But squatted and let the rider pass,
For he wouldn't waste good lead and powder
Just to make the slough-fish and swamp-buzzards prouder
In the land between the rivers.
But he saw the feller's face and thanked his luck
It's the one Pap said was fit to pluck.
So he got on his horse and cantered up the trace.
Called, "Hi thar!" and the stranger watched him coming,
And sat his mare with a smile on his face,
Just watching Little Billie and smiling and humming.
Little Billie rode up and the stranger said,
"Why, bless my heart, if it ain't Little Billie!"

"Good mornen," said Billie, and said, "My Pap
Found somethen you left and knowed you'd be missen,
And Pap don't want nuthen not proper his'n."
But the stranger didn't do a thing but smile and listen
Polite as could be to what Billie said.
But he must have had eyes in the side of his head
As they rode along beside the slough
In the land between the rivers,
Or guessed what Billie was out to do,
For when Billie said, "Mister, I've brung it to you,"
And reached his hand for it down in his britches,
The stranger just reached his own hand, too.

"Boom!" Billie's gun said, and the derringer, "Bang!"
"Oh, I'm shot!" Billie howled and grabbed his shoulder.
"Not bad," said the stranger, "for you're born to hang,
But I'll save some rope 'fore you're a minute older
If you don't high-tail to your honest Pap
In the section between the rivers."
Oh, Billie didn't tarry and Billie didn't linger,
For Billie didn't trust the stranger's finger
And didn't admire the stranger's face
And didn't like the climate of the place,
So he turned and high-tailed up the trace,

With blood on his shirt and snot in his nose
And pee in his pants, for he'd wet his clothes,
And the stranger just sits and admires how he goes,
And says, "Why, that boy would do right well back on the
                                                    Bardstown track!"

"You fool!" said his Pap, but his Mammy cried
To see the place where the gore-blood dried
Round the little hole in her darling's hide.
She wiped his nose and patted his head,
But Pappy barred the door and Pappy said,
"Two hundred in gold's in my money belt,
And take the roan and the brand-new saddle
And stop yore blubberen and skeedaddle,
And next time you try and pull a trick
Fer God's sake don't talk but do it quick."

So Little Billie took his leave
And left his Mammy there to grieve
And left his Pappy in Old Kaintuck
And headed West to try his luck,
For it was Roll, Missouri,
It was Roll, roll, Missouri.
And he was gone nigh ten long year
And never sent word to give his Pappy cheer
Nor wet pen in ink for his Mammy dear.
For Little Billie never was much of a hand with a pen-staff.

(There is always another country and always another place.
There is always another name and another face.
And the name and the face are you, and you
The name and the face, and the stream you gaze into
Will show the adoring face, show the lips that lift to you
As you lean with the implacable thirst of self,
As you lean to the image which is yourself,
To set lip to lip, fix eye on bulging eye,
To drink not of the stream but of your deep identity,
But water is water and it flows,
Under the image on the water the water coils and goes
And its own beginning and its end only the water knows.

*

There are many countries and the rivers in them
—Cumberland, Tennessee, Ohio, Colorado, Pecos, Little Bighorn,
And Roll, Missouri, roll.
But there is only water in them.

And in the new country and in the new place
The eyes of the new friend will reflect the new face
And his mouth will speak to frame
The syllables of the new name
And the name is you and is the agitation of the air
And is the wind and the wind runs and the wind is everywhere.

The name and the face are you.
The name and the face are always new,
But they are you,
And new.

For they have been dipped in the healing flood.
For they have been dipped in the redeeming blood.
For they have been dipped in Time.
For Time is always the new place,
And no-place.
For Time is always the new name and the new face,
And no-name and no-face.

For Time is motion
For Time is innocence
For Time is West.)

Oh, who is coming along the trace,
Whistling along in the late sunshine,
With a big black hat above his big red face
And a long black coat that swings so fine?
Oh, who is riding along the trace
Back to the land between the rivers,
With a big black beard growing down to his guts
And silver mountings on his pistol-butts
And a belt as broad as a saddle-girth
And a look in his eyes like he owned the earth?

293

And meets a man riding up the trace
And squints right sharp and scans his face
And says, "Durn, if it ain't Joe Drew!"
"I reckin it's me," says Joe and gives a spit,
"But whupped if I figger how you knows it,
Fer if I'm Joe, then who air you?"
And the man with the black beard says: "Why, I'm Little Billie!"
And Joe Drew says: "Wal, I'll be whupped."

"Be whupped," Joe said, "and whar you goen?"
"Oh, just visiten back whar I done my growen
In the section between the rivers,
Fer I bin out West and taken my share
And I reckin my luck helt out fer fair,
So I done come home," Little Billie said,
"To see my folks if they ain't dead."
"Ain't dead," Joe answered, and shook his head,
"But that's the best a man kin say,
Fer it looked lak when you went away
You taken West yore Pappy's luck."
Little Billie jingled his pockets and said: "Ain't nuthen wrong with
                                                                    my luck."

And said: "Wal, I'll be gitten on home,
But after yore supper why don't you come
And we'll open a jug and you tell me the news
In the section between the rivers.
But not too early, fer it's my aim
To git me some fun 'fore they know my name,
And tease 'em and fun 'em, fer you never guessed
I was Little Billie that went out West."
And Joe Drew said: "Durn if you always wasn't a hand to git yore fun."

(Over the plain, over mountain and river, drawn,
Wanderer with slit-eyes adjusted to distance,
Drawn out of distance, drawn from the great plateau
Where the sky heeled in the unsagging wind and the cheek burned,
Who stood beneath the white peak that glimmered like a dream,
And spat, and it was morning and it was morning.
You lay among the wild plums and the kildees cried.

You lay in the thicket under the new leaves and the kildees cried,
For all your luck, for all the astuteness of your heart,
And would not stop and would not stop
And the clock ticked all night long in the furnished room
And would not stop
And the *El*-train passed on the quarters with a whish like a terrible broom
And would not stop
And there is always the sound of breathing in the next room
And it will not stop
And the waitress says, "Will that be all, sir, will that be all?"
And will not stop,
For nothing is ever all and nothing is ever all,
For all your experience and your expertness of human vices and of valor
At the hour when the ways are darkened.

Though your luck held and the market was always satisfactory,
Though the letter always came and your lovers were always true,
Though you always received the respect due to your position,
Though your hand never failed of its cunning and your glands always
                                          thoroughly knew their business,
Though your conscience was easy and you were assured of your innocence,
You became gradually aware that something was missing from the picture,

And upon closer inspection exclaimed: "Why, I'm not in it at all!"
Which was perfectly true.
Therefore you tried to remember when you had last had
Whatever it was you had lost,
And you decided to retrace your steps from that point,
But it was a long way back.
It was, nevertheless, absolutely essential to make the effort,
And since you had never been a man to be deterred by difficult
                                          circumstances,

You came back.
For there is no place like home.)

He joked them and teased them and he had his fun
And they never guessed that he was the one
Had been Mammy's darling and Pappy's joy
When he was a great big whickering boy

In the land between the rivers.
He jingled his pockets and took his sop
And patted his belly which was full nigh to pop
And wiped the buttermilk out of his beard
And took his belch and up and reared
Back from the table and cocked his chair
And said: "Old man, ain't you got any fresh drinken water, this here
          ain't fresher'n a hoss puddle?"
And the old woman said: "Pappy, take the young gentleman down to
        the spring so he kin git it good and fresh?"
The old woman gave the old man a straight look.
She gave him the bucket but it was not empty but it was not water.

The stars are shining and the meadow is bright
But under the trees is dark and night
In the land between the rivers.
The leaves hang down in the dark of the trees,
And there is the spring in the dark of the trees,
And there is the spring as black as ink,
And one star in it caught through a chink
Of the leaves that hang down in the dark of the trees.
The star is there but it does not wink.
Little Billie gets down on his knees
And props his hands in the same old place
To sup the water at his ease;
And the star is gone but there is his face.

"Just help yoreself," Big Billie said;
Then set the hatchet in his head.
They went through his pockets and they buried him in the dark
          of the trees.
"I figgered he was a ripe 'un," the old man said.
"Yeah, but you wouldn't done nuthen hadn't bin fer me," the old
         woman said.

(The reflection is shadowy and the form not clear,
For the hour is late, and scarcely a glimmer comes here
Under the leaf, the bough, in innocence dark;
And under your straining face you can scarcely mark
The darkling gleam of your face little less than the water dark.

*

But perhaps what you lost was lost in the pool long ago
When childlike you lost it and then in your innocence rose to go
After kneeling, as now, with your thirst beneath the leaves:
And years it lies here and dreams in the depth and grieves,
More faithful than mother or father in the light or dark of the leaves.

So, weary of greetings now and the new friend's smile,
Weary in art of the stranger, worn with your wanderer's wile,
Weary of innocence and the husks of Time,
You come, back to the homeland of no-Time,
To ask forgiveness and the patrimony of your crime;

And kneel in the untutored night as to demand
What gift—oh, father, father—from that dissevering hand?)

"And whar's Little Billie?" Joe Drew said.
"Air you crazy," said Big, "and plum outa yore head,
Fer you knows he went West nigh ten long year?"
"Went West," Joe said, "but I seen him here
In the section between the rivers,
Riden up the trace as big as you please
With a long black coat comen down to his knees
And a big black beard comen down to his guts
And silver mountens on his pistol-butts,
And he said out West how he done struck
It rich and wuz bringen you back your luck."
"I shore-God could use some luck," Big Billie said,
But his woman wet her lips and craned her head,
And said: "Come riden with a big black beard, you say?"
And Joe: "Oh, it wuz Billie as big as day."

And the old man's eyes bugged out of a sudden and he croaked like a
          sick bull-frog and said: "Come riden with a long black coat?"

The night is still and the grease-lamp low
And the old man's breath comes wheeze and slow.
Oh, the blue flame sucks on the old rag wick
And the old woman's breath comes sharp and quick,
And there isn't a sound under the roof

But her breath's hiss and his breath's puff,
And there isn't a sound outside the door
As they hearken but cannot hear any more
The creak of saddle or the plop of hoof,
For a long time now Joe Drew's been gone
And left them sitting there alone
In the land between the rivers.
And so they sit and breathe and wait
And breathe while the night gets big and late,
And neither of them gives move or stir.
She won't look at him and he won't look at her.
He doesn't look at her but he says: "Git me the spade."

She grabbled with her hands and he dug with the spade
Where leaves let down the dark and shade
In the land between the rivers.
She grabbled like a dog in the hole they made,
But stopped of a sudden and then she said,
"My hand's on his face."
They light up a pine-knot and lean at the place
Where the man in the black coat slumbers and lies
With trash in his beard and dirt on his face;
And the torch-flame shines in his wide-open eyes.
Down the old man leans with the flickering flame
And moves his lips, says: "Tell me his name."

"Ain't Billie, ain't Billie," the old woman cries,
"Oh, it ain't my Billie, fer he wuz little
And helt to my skirt while I stirred the kittle
And called me Mammy and hugged me tight
And come in the house when it fell night."
But the old man leans down with the flickering flame
And croaks: "But tell me his name."

"Oh, he ain't got none, he jist come riden
From some fer place whar he'd bin biden.
Ain't got a name and never had none—
But Billie, my Billie, he had one,
And hit was Billie, it was his name."
But the old man croaked: "Tell me his name."

*

"Oh, he ain't got none and it's all the same,
But Billie had one, and he was little
And offen his chin I would wipe the spittle
And wiped the drool and kissed him thar
And counted his toes and kissed him whar
The little black mark was under his tit,
Shaped lak a clover under his left tit,
With a shape fer luck, and I'd kiss hit—"

The old man blinks in the pine-knot flare
And his mouth comes open like a fish for air,
Then he says right low, "I had nigh fergot."
"Oh, I kissed him on his little luck-spot
And I kissed and he'd laugh as lak as not—"
The old man said: "Git his shirt open."
The old woman opened the shirt and there was the birthmark under
the left tit.

It was shaped for luck.

(The bee knows, and the eel's cold ganglia burn.
And the sad head lifting to the long return,
Through brumal deeps, in the great unsolsticed coil,
Carries its knowledge, navigator without star,
And under the stars, pure in its clamorous toil,
The goose hoots north where the starlit marshes are.
The salmon heaves at the fall, and, wanderer, you
Heave at the great fall of Time, and gorgeous, gleam
In the powerful arc, and anger and outrage like dew,
In your plunge, fling, and plunge to the thunderous stream:
Back to the silence, back to the pool, back
To the high pool, motionless, and the unmurmuring dream.
And you, wanderer, back,
Brother to pinion and the pious fin that cleave
The innocence of air and the disinfectant flood
And wing and welter and weave
The long compulsion and the circuit hope
Back,

And bear through that limitless and devouring fluidity
The itch and humble promise which is home.

*

And the father waits for the son.

The hour is late,
The scene familiar even in shadow,
The transaction brief,
And you, wanderer, back,
After the striving and the wind's word,
To kneel
Here in the evening empty of wind or bird,
To kneel in the sacramental silence of evening
At the feet of the old man
Who is evil and ignorant and old,
To kneel
With the little black mark under your heart,
Which is your name,
Which is shaped for luck,

Which is your luck.)

Original Sin: A Short Story

Nodding, its great head rattling like a gourd,
And locks like seaweed strung on the stinking stone,
The nightmare stumbles past, and you have heard
It fumble your door before it whimpers and is gone:
It acts like the old hound that used to snuffle your door and moan.

You thought you had lost it when you left Omaha,
For it seemed connected then with your grandpa, who
Had a wen on his forehead and sat on the veranda
To finger the precious protuberance, as was his habit to do,
Which glinted in sun like rough garnet or the rich old brain
                                               bulging through.

But you met it in Harvard Yard as the historic steeple
Was confirming the midnight with its hideous racket,
And you wondered how it had come, for its stood so imbecile,
With empty hands, humble, and surely nothing in pocket:
Riding the rods, perhaps—or Grandpa's will paid the ticket.

You were almost kindly then, in your first homesickness,
As it tortured its stiff face to speak, but scarcely mewed.
Since then you have outlived all your homesickness,
But have met it in many another distempered latitude:
Oh, nothing is lost, ever lost! at last you understood.

It never came in the quantum glare of sun
To shame you before your friends, and had nothing to do
With your public experience or private reformation:
But it thought no bed too narrow—it stood with lips askew
And shook it's great head sadly like the abstract Jew.

Never met you in the lyric arsenical meadow
When children call and your heart goes stone in the bosom—
At the orchard anguish never, nor ovoid horror,

Which is furred like a peach or avid like the delicious plum.
It takes no part in your classic prudence or fondled axiom.

Not there when you exclaimed: "Hope is betrayed by
Disastrous glory of sea-capes, sun-torment of whitecaps
—There must be a new innocence for us to be stayed by."
But there it stood, after all the timetables, all the maps,
In the crepuscular clutter of *always, always,* or *perhaps.*

You have moved often and rarely left an address,
And hear of the deaths of friends with a sly pleasure,
A sense of cleansing and hope which blooms from distress;
But it has not died, it comes, its hand childish, unsure,
Clutching the bribe of chocolate or a toy you used to treasure.

It tries the lock. You hear, but simply drowse:
There is nothing remarkable in that sound at the door.
Later you may hear it wander the dark house
Like a mother who rises at night to seek a childhood picture;
Or it goes to the backyard and stands like an old horse cold in the pasture.

Eidolon

All night, in May, dogs barked in the hollow woods;
Hoarse, from secret huddles of no light,
By moonlit bole, hoarse, the dogs gave tongue.
In May, by moon, no moon, thus: I remember
Of their far clamor the throaty, infatuate timbre.

The boy, all night, lay in the black room,
Tick-straw, all night, harsh to the bare side.
Staring, he heard; the clotted dark swam slow.
Far off, by wind, no wind, unappeasable riot
Provoked, resurgent, the bosom's nocturnal disquiet.

What hungers kept the house? under the rooftree
The boy; the man, clod-heavy, hard hand uncurled;
The old man, eyes wide, spittle on his beard.
In dark was crushed the may-apple: plunging, the rangers
Of dark remotelier belled their unhouseled angers.

Dogs quartered the black woods: blood black on
May-apple at dawn, old beech-husk. And trails are lost
By rock, in ferns lost, by pools unlit.
I heard the hunt. Who saw, in darkness, how fled
The white eidolon from the fangèd commotion rude?

Revelation

Because he had spoken harshly to his mother,
The day became astonishingly bright,
The enormity of distance crept to him like a dog now,
And earth's own luminescence seemed to repel the night.

Rent was the roof like loud paper to admit
Sun-sulphurous splendor where had been before
But a submarine glimmer by kindly countenances lit,
As slow, phosphorescent dignities light the ocean floor.

By walls, by walks, chrysanthemum and aster,
All hairy, fat-petaled species, lean, confer,
And his ears, and heart, should burn at that insidious whisper
Which concerns him so, he knows; but he cannot make out the words.

The peacock screamed, and his feathered fury made
Legend shake, all day, while the sky ran pale as milk;
That night, all night, the buck rabbit stamped in the moonlit glade,
And the owl's brain glowed like a coal in the grove's combustible dark.

When Sulla smote and Rome was racked, Augustine
Recalled how Nature, shuddering, tore her gown,
And kind changed kind, and the blunt herbivorous tooth dripped blood;
At Inverness, at Duncan's death, chimneys blew down.

But, oh! his mother was kinder than ever Rome,
Dearer than Duncan—no wonder, then, Nature's frame
Thrilled in voluptuous hemispheres far off from his home;
But not in terror: only as the bride, as the bride.

In separateness only does love learn definition,
Though Brahma smiles beneath the dappled shade,
Though tears, that night, wet the pillow where the boy's head was laid,
Dreamless of splendid antipodal agitation;

*

And though across what tide and tooth Time is,
He was to lean back toward that irredeemable face,
He would think, than Sulla more fortunate, how once he had learned
Something important above love, and about love's grace.

Bearded Oaks

The oaks, how subtle and marine,
Bearded, and all the layered light
Above them swims; and thus the scene,
Recessed, awaits the positive night.

So, waiting, we in the grass now lie
Beneath the languorous tread of light:
The grasses, kelp-like, satisfy
The nameless motions of the air.

Upon the floor of light, and time,
Unmurmuring, of polyp made,
We rest; we are, as light withdraws,
Twin atolls on a shelf of shade.

Ages to our construction went,
Dim architecture, hour by hour:
And violence, forgot now, lent
The present stillness all its power.

The storm of noon above us rolled,
Of light the fury, furious gold,
The long drag troubling us, the depth:
Dark is unrocking, unrippling, still.

Passion and slaughter, ruth, decay
Descend, minutely whispering down,
Silted down swaying streams, to lay
Foundation for our voicelessness.

All our debate is voiceless here,
As all our rage, the rage of stone;
If hope is hopeless, then fearless is fear,
And history is thus undone.

*

Our feet once wrought the hollow street
With echo when the lamps were dead
At windows, once our headlight glare
Disturbed the doe that, leaping, fled.

I do not love you less that now
The caged heart makes iron stroke,
Or less that all that light once gave
The graduate dark should now revoke.

We live in time so little time
And we learn all so painfully,
That we may spare this hour's term
To practice for eternity.

Picnic Remembered

That day, so innocent appeared
The leaf, the hill, the sky, to us,
Their structures so harmonious
And pure, that all we had endured
Seemed the quaint disaster of a child,
Now cupboarded, and all the wild
Grief canceled; so with what we feared.

We stood among the painted trees:
The amber light laved them, and us;
Or light then so untremulous,
So steady, that our substances,
Twin flies, were as in amber tamed
With our perfections stilled and framed
To mock Time's marveling after-spies.

Joy, strongest medium, then buoyed
Us when we moved, as swimmers, who,
Relaxed, resign them to the flow
And pause of their unstained flood.
Thus wrapped, sustained, we did not know
How darkness darker staired below;
Or knowing, but half understood.

The bright deception of that day!
When we so readily could gloze
All pages opened to expose
The trust we never would betray;
But darkness on the landscape grew
As in our bosoms darkness, too;
And that was what we took away.

*

And it abides, and may abide:
Though ebbed from the region happier mapped,
Our hearts, like hollow stones, have trapped
A corner of that brackish tide.
The jaguar breath, the secret wrong,
The curse that curls the sudden tongue,
We know; for fears have fructified.

Or are we dead, that we, unmanned,
Are vacant, and our clearest souls
Are sped where each with each patrols,
In still society, hand in hand,
That scene where we, too, wandered once
Who now inherit a new province:
Love's limbo, this lost under-land?

The *then*, the *now*: each cenotaph
Of the other, and proclaims it dead.
Or is the soul a hawk that, fled
On glimmering wings past vision's path,
Reflects the last gleam to us here
Though sun is sunk and darkness near
—Uncharted Truth's high heliograph?

The Garden

On prospect of a fine day in early autumn

How kind, how secret, now the sun
Will bless this garden frost has won,
And touch once more, as once it used,
The furled boughs by cold bemused.
Though summered brilliance had but room
In blossom, now the leaves will bloom
Their time, and take from milder sun
An unreviving benison.

   No marbles whitely gaze among
These paths where gilt the late pear hung:
But branches interlace to frame
The avenue of stately flame
Where yonder, far more bold and pure
Than marble, gleams the sycamore,
Of argent torse and cunning shaft
Propped nobler than the sculptor's craft.

   The hand that crooked upon the spade
Here plucked the peach, and thirst allayed;
Here lovers paused before the kiss,
Instructed of what ripeness is:
Where all who came might stand to prove
The grace of this imperial grove,
Now jay and cardinal debate,
Like twin usurpers, the ruined state.

   But he who sought, not love, but peace
In such rank plot could take no ease:
Now poised between the two alarms
Of summer's lusts and winter's harms,
Only for him these precincts wait
In sacrament that can translate
All things that fed luxurious sense
From appetite to innocence.

The Return: An Elegy

The east wind finds the gap bringing rain:
Rain in the pine wind shaking the stiff pine.
Beneath the wind the hollow gorges whine.
The pines decline.
Slow film of rain creeps own the loam again
Where the blind and nameless bones recline.

    all are conceded to the earth's absolute chemistry
    they burn like faggots in—of damp and dark—the monstrous
                                bulging flame.

    calcium phosphate lust speculation faith treachery
    it walked upright with habitation and a name

       tell me its name

The pines, black, like combers plunge with spray
Lick the wind's unceasing keel.
It is not long till day
The boughs like hairy swine in slaughter squeal.
They lurch beneath the thunder's livid heel.
The pines, black, snore *what does the wind say?*

       tell me its name

I have a name: I am not blind.
Eyes, not blind, press to the Pullman pane
Survey the driving dark and silver taunt of rain.
What will I find
What will I find beyond the snoring pine?
O eyes locked blind in death's immaculate design
Shall fix their last distrust in mine.

    give me the nickels off your eyes
    from your hands the violets

311

let me bless your obsequies
if you possessed conveniently enough three eyes
then I could buy a pack of cigarettes

In gorges where the dead fox lies the fern
Will rankest loop the battened frond and fall
Above the bare tushed jaws that turn
Their insolence unto the gracious catafalque and pall.
It will be the season when milkweed blossoms burn.

the old bitch is dead
what have I said!
I have only said what the wind said
wind shakes a bell the hollow head

By dawn, the wind, the blown rain
Will cease their antique concitation.
It is the hour when old ladies cough and wake,
The chair, the table, take their form again
And earth begins the matinal exhalation.

does my mother wake

Pines drip without motion.
The hairy boughs no longer shake.
Shaggy mist, crookbacked, ascends.
Round hairy boughs the mist with shaggy fingers bends.
No wind: no rain:
Why do the steady pines complain?
Complain

the old fox is dead
what have I said

Locked in the roaring cubicle
Over the mountains through darkness hurled
I race the daylight's westward cycle
Across the groaning rooftree of the world.
The mist is furled.

*

a hundred years they took this road
the lank hunters then men hard-eyed with hope:
ox breath whitened the chill air: the goad
fell: here on the western slope
the hungry people the lost ones took their abode
here they took their stand:
alders bloomed on the road to the new land
here is the house the broken door the shed
the old fox is dead

The wheels hum hum
The wheels: I come I come.
Whirl out of space through time O wheels
Pursue down backward time the ghostly parallels
Pursue past culvert cut embankment semaphore
Pursue down gleaming hours that are no more.
The pines, black, snore

    turn backward turn backward O time in your flight
    and make me a child again just for tonight
    good lord he's wet the bed come bring a light

What grief has the mind distilled?
The heart is unfulfilled
The hoarse pine stilled.
I cannot pluck
Out of this land of pine and rock
Of red bud their season not yet gone
If I could pluck
(In drouth the lizard will blink on the hot limestone)

    the old fox is dead
    what is said is said
    heaven rest the hoary head
    what have I said!
    ... I have only said what the wind said
    honor thy father and mother in the days of thy youth
    for time uncoils like the cottonmouth

*

If I could pluck
Out of the dark that whirled
Over the hoarse pine over the rock
Out of the mist that furled
Could I stretch forth like God the hand and gather
For you my mother
If I could pluck
Against the dry essential of tomorrow
To lay upon the breast that gave me suck
Out of the dark the dark and swollen orchid of this sorrow.

Kentucky Mountain Farm

I. REBUKE OF THE ROCKS

Now on you is the hungry equinox,
O little stubborn people of the hill,
The season of the obscene moon whose pull
Disturbs the sod, the rabbit, the lank fox,
Moving the waters, the boar's dull blood,
And the acrid sap of the ironwood.

But breed no tender thing among the rocks.
Rocks are too old under the mad moon,
Renouncing passion by the strength that locks
The eternal agony of fire in stone.

Then quit yourselves as stone and cease
To break the weary stubble-field for seed;
Let not the naked cattle bear increase,
Let barley wither and the bright milkweed.
Instruct the heart, lean men, of a rocky place
That even the little flesh and fevered bone
May keep the sweet sterility of stone.

II. AT THE HOUR OF THE BREAKING OF THE ROCKS

Beyond the wrack and eucharist of snow
The tortured and reluctant rock again
Receives the sunlight and the tarnished rain.
Such is the hour of sundering we know,
Who on the hills have seen stand and pass
Stubbornly the taciturn
Lean men that of all things alone
Were, not as water or the febrile grass,
Figured in kinship to the savage stone.

*

315

The hills are weary, the lean men have passed;
The rocks are stricken, and the frost has torn
Away their ridged fundaments at last,
So that the fractured atoms now are borne
Down shifting waters to the tall, profound
Shadow of the absolute deeps,
Wherein the spirit moves and never sleeps
That held the foot among the rocks, that bound
The tired hand upon the stubborn plow,
Knotted the flesh unto the hungry bone,
The redbud to the charred and broken bough,
And strung the bitter tendons of the stone.

III. HISTORY AMONG THE ROCKS

There are many ways to die
Here among the rocks in any weather:
Wind, down the eastern gap, will lie
Level along the snow, beating the cedar,
And lull the drowsy head that it blows over
To startle a cold and crystalline dream forever.

The hound's black paw will print the grass in May,
And sycamores rise down a dark ravine,
Where a creek in flood, sucking the rock and clay,
Will tumble the laurel, the sycamore away.
Think how a body, naked and lean
And white as the splintered sycamore, would go
Tumbling and turning, hushed in the end,
With hair afloat in waters that gently bend
To ocean where the blind tides flow.

Under the shadow of ripe wheat,
By flat limestone, will coil the copperhead,
Fanged as the sunlight, hearing the reaper's feet.
But there are other ways, the lean men said:
In these autumn orchards once young men lay dead—
Gray coats, blue coats. Young men on the mountainside

Clambered, fought. Heels muddied the rocky spring.
Their reason is hard to guess, remembering
Blood on their black mustaches in moonlight.
Their reason is hard to guess and a long time past:
The apple falls, falling in the quiet night.

IV. WATERSHED

From this high place all things flow.
Land of divided streams, of water spilled
Eastward, westward, without memento . . .
Land where the morning mist is furled
Like smoke above the ridgepole of the world.

The sunset hawk now rides
The tall light up the climbing deep of air.
Beneath him swings the rooftree that divides
The east and west. His gold eyes scan
The crumpled shade on gorge and crest
And streams that creep and disappear, appear,
Past fingered ridges and their shrivelling span.
Under the broken eaves men take their rest.

Forever, should they stir, their thought would keep
This place. Not love, happiness past, constrains,
But certitude. Enough, and it remains,
Though they who thread the flood and neap
Of earth itself have felt the earth creep;
In pastures hung against the rustling gorge
Have felt the shuddering and sweat of stone,
Knowing thereby no constant moon
Sustains the hill's lost granite surge.

V. THE RETURN

Burly and clean, with bark in umber scrolled
About the sunlit bole's own living white,
The sycamore stood, drenched in the autumn light.
The same old tree. Again the timeless gold

Broad leaf released the tendoned bough, and slow,
Uncertain as a casual memory,
Wavered aslant the ripe unmoving air.
Up from the whiter bough, the bluer sky,
That glimmered in the water's depth below,
A richer leaf rose to the other there.
They touched; with the gentle clarity of dream,
Bosom to bosom, burned, one on, one in, the quiet stream.

But, backward heart, you have no voice to call
Your image back, the vagrant image again.
The tree, the leaf falling, the stream, and all
Familiar faithless things would yet remain
Voiceless. And he, who had loved as well as most,
Might have foretold it thus, for well he knew
How, glimmering, a buried world is lost
In the water's riffle or the wind's flaw;
How his own image, perfect and deep
And small within loved eyes, had been forgot,
Her face being turned, or when those eyes were shut
Past light in that fond accident of sleep.

Pondy Woods

The buzzards over Pondy Woods
Achieve the blue tense altitudes,
Black figments that the woods release,
Obscenity in form and grace,
Drifting high through the pure sunshine
Till the sun in gold decline.

Big Jim Todd was a slick black buck
Laying low in the mud and muck
Of Pondy Woods when the sun went down
In gold, and the buzzards tilted down
A windless vortex to the black-gum trees
To sit along the quiet boughs,
Devout and swollen, at their ease.

By the buzzard roost Big Jim Todd
Listened for hoofs on the corduroy road
Or for the foul and sucking sound
A man's foot makes on the marshy ground.
Past midnight, when the moccasin
Slipped from the log and, trailing in
Its obscured waters, broke
The dark algae, one lean bird spoke.

"Nigger, you went this afternoon
For your Saturday spree at the Blue Goose saloon,
So you've got on your Sunday clothes,
On your big splay feet got patent-leather shoes.
But a buzzard can smell the thing you've done;
The posse will get you—run, nigger, run—
There's a fellow behind you with a big shot-gun.
Nigger, nigger, you'll sweat cold sweat
In your patent-leather shoes and Sunday clothes
When down your track the steeljacket goes
Mean and whimpering over the wheat.

*

"Nigger, your breed ain't metaphysical."
The buzzard coughed. His words fell
In the darkness, mystic and ambrosial.
"But we maintain our ancient rite,
Eat the gods by day and prophesy by night.
We swing against the sky and wait;
You seize the hour, more passionate
Than strong, and strive with time to die—
With Time, the beaked tribe's astute ally.

"The Jew-boy died. The Syrian vulture swung
Remotely above the cross whereon he hung
From dinner-time to supper-time, and all
The people gathered there watched him until
The lean brown chest no longer stirred,
Then idly watched the slow majestic bird
That in the last sun above the twilit hill
Gleamed for a moment at the height and slid
Down the hot wind and in the darkness hid.
Nigger, regard the circumstance of breath:
Non omnis moriar, the poet saith."

Pedantic, the bird clacked its gray beak,
With a Tennessee accent to the classic phrase;
Jim understood, and was about to speak,
But the buzzard drooped one wing and filmed the eyes.

At dawn unto the Sabbath wheat he came,
That gave to the dew its faithless yellow flame
From kindly loam in recollection of
The fires that in the brutal rock once strove.
To the ripe wheat fields he came at dawn.
Northward the printed smoke stood quiet above
The distant cabins of Squiggtown.
A train's far whistle blew and drifted away
Coldly; lucid and thin the morning lay
Along the farms, and here no sound
Touched the sweet earth miraculously stilled.
Then down the damp and sudden wood there belled
The musical white-throated hound.

*

320

In Pondy Woods in the summer's drouth
Lurk fever and the cottonmouth.
And buzzards over Pondy Woods
Achieve the blue tense altitudes,
Drifting high in the pure sunshine
Till the sun in gold decline;
Then golden and hieratic through
The night their eyes burn two by two.

To a Face in a Crowd

Brother, my brother, whither do you pass?
Unto what hill at dawn, unto what glen,
Where among the rocks the faint lascivious grass
Fingers in lust the arrogant bones of men?

Beside what bitter waters will you go
Where the lean gulls of your heart along the shore
Rehearse to the cliffs the rhetoric of their woe?
In dream, perhaps, I have seen your face before.

A certain night has borne both you and me;
We are the children of an ancient band
Broken between the mountains and the sea.
A cromlech marks for you that utmost strand

And you must find the dolorous place they stood.
Of old I know that shore, that dim terrain,
And know how black and turbulent the blood
Will beat through iron chambers of the brain

When at your back the taciturn tall stone,
Which is your fathers' monument and mark,
Repeats the waves' implacable monotone,
Ascends the night and propagates the dark.

Men there have lived who wrestled with the ocean;
I was afraid—the polyp was their shroud.
I was afraid. That shore of your decision
Awaits beyond this street where in the crowd

Your face is blown, an apparition, past.
Renounce the night as I, and we must meet
As weary nomads in this desert at last,
Borne in the lost procession of these feet.

ABOUT THE AUTHOR

ROBERT PENN WARREN was born in Guthrie, Kentucky, in 1905. After graduating summa cum laude from Vanderbilt University (1925), he received a master's degree from the University of California (1927), and did graduate work at Yale University (1927–28) and at Oxford as a Rhodes Scholar (B. Litt., 1930).

Mr. Warren has published many books, including ten novels, sixteen volumes of poetry, and a volume of short stories; also a play, a collection of critical essays, a biography, three historical essays, a critical book on Dreiser and a study of Melville, and two studies of race relations in America. This body of work has been published in a period of fifty-three years—a period during which Mr. Warren also had an active career as a professor of English.

All the King's Men (1946) was awarded the Pulitzer Prize for Fiction. The Shelley Memorial Award recognized Mr. Warren's early poems. *Promises* (1957) won the Pulitzer Prize for Poetry, the Edna St. Vincent Millay Prize for the Poetry Society of America, and the National Book Award. In 1944–45 Mr. Warren was the second occupant of the Chair of Poetry at the Library of Congress. In 1952 he was elected to the American Philosophical Society; in 1959 to the American Academy of Arts and Letters; and in 1975 to the American Academy of Arts and Sciences. In 1967 he received the Bollingen Prize in Poetry for *Selected Poems: New and Old, 1923–1966*, and in 1970 the National Medal for Literature, and the Van Wyck Brooks Award for the book-length poem *Audubon: A Vision*. In 1974 he was chosen by the National Endowment for the Humanities to deliver the third Annual Jefferson Lecture in the Humanities. In 1975 he received the Emerson-Thoreau Award of the American Academy of Arts and Sciences. In 1976 he received the Copernicus Award from the Academy of American Poets, in recognition of his career but with special notice of *Or Else—Poem/Poems 1968–1974*. In 1977 he received the Harriet Monroe Prize for Poetry and the Wilma and Roswell Messing, Jr. Award. In 1979, for *Now and Then*, a book of new poems, he received his third Pulitzer Prize. In 1980 he received the Award of the Connecticut Arts Council, the Presidential Medal of Freedom, the Common Wealth Award for Literature, and the Hubbell Memorial Award (The Modern Language Association). In 1981 he was a recipient of a Prize Fellowship of the John D. and Catherine T. MacArthur Foundation.

Mr. Warren lives in Connecticut with his wife, Eleanor Clark (author of *The Bitter Box, Rome and a Villa, The Oysters of Locmariaquer, Baldur's Gate, Eyes, Etc.: A Memoir*, and *Gloria Mundi*). They have two children, Rosanna and Gabriel.

DATE DUE

DEC 12 '88			
APR 14 '87			
DEC 21 1989			
DEC 15 89			
GAYLORD			PRINTED IN U.S.A.